TEACHING STUDENTS
WITH
MEDICAL, PHYSICAL,
AND
MULTIPLE DISABILITIES

A Practical Approach to Special Education for Every Teacher

The Fundamentals of Special Education
A Practical Guide for Every Teacher

The Legal Foundations of Special Education
A Practical Guide for Every Teacher

Effective Assessment for Students With Special Needs
A Practical Guide for Every Teacher

Effective Instruction for Students With Special Needs
A Practical Guide for Every Teacher

Working With Families and Community Agencies to Support Students With Special Needs
A Practical Guide for Every Teacher

Public Policy, School Reform, and Special Education
A Practical Guide for Every Teacher

Teaching Students With Sensory Disabilities
A Practical Guide for Every Teacher

Teaching Students With Medical, Physical, and Multiple Disabilities
A Practical Guide for Every Teacher

Teaching Students With Learning Disabilities
A Practical Guide for Every Teacher

Teaching Students With Communication Disorders
A Practical Guide for Every Teacher

Teaching Students With Emotional Disturbance
A Practical Guide for Every Teacher

Teaching Students With Mental Retardation
A Practical Guide for Every Teacher

Teaching Students With Gifts and Talents
A Practical Guide for Every Teacher

TEACHING STUDENTS
WITH
MEDICAL, PHYSICAL,
AND
MULTIPLE DISABILITIES

A Practical Guide for Every Teacher

BOB ALGOZZINE
JIM YSSELDYKE

CORWIN PRESS
A SAGE Publications Company
Thousand Oaks, California

For information:

Corwin Press
A Sage Publications Company
2455 Teller Road
Thousand Oaks, California 91320
www.corwinpress.com

Sage Publications Ltd.
1 Oliver's Yard
55 City Road
London EC1Y 1SP
United Kingdom

Sage Publications India Pvt. Ltd.
B-42, Panchsheel Enclave
Post Box 4109
New Delhi 110 017 India

Printed in the United States of America

Library of Congress Cataloging-in-Publication Data

Algozzine, Robert.
Teaching students with medical, physical, and multiple disabilities:
A practical guide for every teacher / Bob Algozzine & James E. Ysseldyke.
    p. cm.
Includes bibliographical references and index.
ISBN 1-4129-3948-8 (cloth : alk. paper)
ISBN 1-4129-3901-1 (pbk. : alk. paper)
    1. Children with disabilities—Education—United States. 2. Children with mental disabilities—Education—United States. 3. Special education—United States. 4. Special education teachers—Training of—United States. I. Ysseldyke, James E. II. Title.
LC4031.A56 2006
371.91—dc22

2005037824

This book is printed on acid-free paper.

06 07 08 09 10 9 8 7 6 5 4 3 2 1

Acquisitions Editor:	Kylee M. Liegl
Editorial Assistant:	Nadia Kashper
Production Editor:	Denise Santoyo
Copy Editor:	Karen E. Taylor
Typesetter:	C&M Digitals (P) Ltd.
Indexer:	Kathy Paparchontis
Cover Designer:	Michael Dubowe

Contents

About
A Practical Approach to Special Education for Every Teacher

Special education means specially designed instruction for students with unique learning needs. Students receive special education for many reasons. Students with disabilities such as mental retardation, hearing impairments (including deafness), speech or language impairments, visual impairments (including blindness), emotional disturbance, orthopedic impairments, autism, traumatic brain injury, other health impairments, or specific learning disabilities are entitled to special education services. Students who are gifted and talented also receive special education. Special education services are delivered in many settings, including regular classes, resource rooms, and separate classes. The 13 books of this collection will help you teach students with disabilities and those with gifts and talents. Each book focuses on a specific area of special education and can be used individually or in conjunction with all or some of the other books. Six of the books provide the background and content knowledge you need in order to work effectively with all students with unique learning needs:

Book 1: The Fundamentals of Special Education

Book 2: The Legal Foundations of Special Education

Book 3: Effective Assessment for Students With Special Needs

Book 4: Effective Instruction for Students With Special Needs

Book 5: Working With Families and Community Agencies to Support Students With Special Needs

Book 6: Public Policy, School Reform, and Special Education

Seven of the books focus on teaching specific groups of students who receive special education:

Book 7:   Teaching Students With Sensory Disabilities

Book 8:   Teaching Students With Medical, Physical, and Multiple Disabilities

Book 9:   Teaching Students With Learning Disabilities

Book 10: Teaching Students With Communication Disorders

Book 11: Teaching Students With Emotional Disturbance

Book 12: Teaching Students With Mental Retardation

Book 13: Teaching Students With Gifts and Talents

All of the books in *A Practical Approach to Special Education for Every Teacher* will help you to make a difference in the lives of all students, especially those with unique learning needs.

ACKNOWLEDGMENTS

The approach we take in *A Practical Approach to Special Education for Every Teacher* is an effort to change how professionals learn about special education. The 13 separate books are a result of prodding from our students and from professionals in the field to provide a set of materials that "cut to the chase" in teaching them about students with disabilities and about building the capacity of systems to meet those students' needs. Teachers told us that in their classes they always confront students with special learning needs and students their school district has assigned a label to (e.g., students with learning disabilities). Our students and the professionals we worked with wanted a very practical set of texts that gave them the necessary **information** *about* **the students** (e.g., federal definitions, student characteristics) and specific **information on** *what to do about* **the students** (assessment and teaching strategies, approaches that work). They also wanted the opportunity to purchase parts of textbooks, rather than entire texts, to learn what they needed.

The production of this collection would not have been possible without the support and assistance of many colleagues. Professionals associated with Corwin Press—Faye Zucker, Kylee Liegl, Robb Clouse—helped us work through the idea of introducing special education differently, and their support in helping us do it is deeply appreciated.

Faye Ysseldyke and Kate Algozzine, our children, and our grandchildren also deserve recognition. They have made the problems associated with the project very easy to diminish, deal with, or dismiss. Every day in every way, they enrich our lives and make us better. We are grateful for them.

About the Authors

Bob Algozzine, PhD, is Professor in the Department of Educational Leadership at the University of North Carolina at Charlotte and project codirector of the U.S. Department of Education–supported Behavior and Reading Improvement Center. With 25 years of research experience and extensive first-hand knowledge of teaching students classified as seriously emotionally disturbed (and other equally useless terms), Algozzine is a uniquely qualified staff developer, conference speaker, and teacher of behavior management and effective teaching courses.

As an active partner and collaborator with professionals in the Charlotte-Mecklenburg schools in North Carolina and as an editor of several journals focused on special education, Algozzine keeps his finger on the pulse of current special education practice. He has written more than 250 manuscripts on special education topics, authoring many popular books and textbooks on how to manage emotional and social behavior problems. Through *A Practical Approach to Special Education for Every Teacher,* Algozzine hopes to continue to help improve the lives of students with special needs—and the professionals who teach them.

Jim Ysseldyke, PhD, is Birkmaier Professor in the Department of Educational Psychology, director of the School Psychology Program, and director of the Center for Reading Research at the University of Minnesota. Widely requested as a staff developer and conference speaker, he brings more than 30 years of research and teaching experience to educational professionals around the globe.

As the former director of the federally funded National Center on Educational Outcomes, Ysseldyke conducted research and provided technical support that helped to boost the academic performance of students with disabilities and improve school assessment techniques nationally. Today he continues to work to improve the education of students with disabilities.

The author of more than 300 publications on special education and school psychology, Ysseldyke is best known for his textbooks on assessment, effective instruction, issues in special education, and other cutting-edge areas of education and school psychology. With *A Practical Approach to Special Education for Every Teacher*, he seeks to equip educators with practical knowledge and methods that will help them to better engage students in exploring—and meeting—all their potentials.

Self-Assessment 1

Before you begin this book, check your knowledge of the content being covered. Choose the best answer for each of the following questions.

1. Students who have limited strength, vitality, or alertness that adversely affects their educational performance are called

    a. medically fragile

    b. other health impaired

    c. medically impaired

    d. physically impaired

2. The number of students with health impairments receiving special education services during the past ten years has

    a. increased

    b. remained constant

    c. decreased

    d. first decreased then gradually increased

3. Any _____ that interferes with learning and achievement at school can make students eligible for special services under the category of other health impairments.

    a. physical disability

    b. emotional disability

    c. cognitive disorder

    d. disease

4. Charles has a hereditary disease that affects the lungs and the pancreas. He has recurring respiratory and digestive problems. This disease is

   a. muscular dystrophy

   b. epilepsy

   c. cystic fibrosis

   d. multiple sclerosis

5. Tyrell has a hereditary disease that results in his bleeding excessively from minor cuts and scrapes. He also suffers from internal bleeding if he gets a bruise. This disease is

   a. hemophilia

   b. epilepsy

   c. poliomyelitis

   d. multiple sclerosis

6. A group of birth disorders in which the skeletal muscles progressively deteriorate is called

   a. epilepsy

   b. muscular dystrophy

   c. cerebral palsy

   d. polio

7. Students who require specialized technological health care procedures for life support or health support during the school day are called

   a. technology dependent

   b. dependent

   c. medically fragile

   d. medically dependent

8. Individuals who depend on life-sustaining medical equipment and complex nursing care to avoid death or further disabilities are called

   a. technology dependent

   b. dependent

   c. medically fragile

   d. medically dependent

9. Impairments that involve the muscular, skeletal, and possibly the central nervous systems are

   a. orthopedic

   b. traumatic

   c. acquired

   d. voluntary

10. William suffered a severe head injury when he was hit by a car while riding his bicycle. He was not wearing the bicycle helmet that his parents had purchased for him. As a result of that injury, William has had chronic problems affecting his achievement at school, his behavior, and his social skills. This injury is referred to as

    a. orthopedic impairment

    b. traumatic brain injury

    c. acquired immune disorder

    d. craniofacial anomalies

REFLECTION

After you answer the multiple-choice questions, think about how you would answer to the following questions:

- What factors might affect the academic success of individuals with medical disabilities?
- What factors might affect the academic success of individuals with orthopedic impairments?
- What do effective teachers do to provide support for students with medical disabilities?

Introduction to Teaching Students With Medical, Physical, and Multiple Disabilities

"I can't believe I won the scholarship. I mean I thought the story I wrote was good, but not that good." **Martin** is a 17-year-old high school junior. He has cerebral palsy, a condition that restricts his speech and coordination. He uses crutches to get around school, but requires very little assistance during the school day. All of his instruction is provided in classes with his neighbors and peers. A special education teacher supports Martin's teachers whenever they request help. Martin uses a computer to communicate with his teachers and peers.

"For years we went to the same school, and it wasn't easy being the younger sister of the only person in the school with a disability. Everybody knew me as, Bonnie, Mavis's sister. I thought I had to protect her, and when she told me she wanted to take care of herself, life got a lot easier." Because **Mavis** was born without feet, getting around is not easy for her. Although Bonnie wishes her family could do more physical activities together, she realizes it probably wouldn't happen even if Mavis didn't have a disability. After all, regardless of physical characteristics, family members don't always share common interests. And disabilities don't have to control a person's life.

(Continued)

(Continued)

"A lot of people would back away from me on the street. They would actually run away from me. People who associated with me were not treated much better." **Ryan** did not look different from the other boys in his class. He didn't act much differently either. But Ryan's medical condition was unlike anything his peers ever experienced. Ryan had hemophilia; his body lacked a substance needed to make his blood clot. If he was cut or even bruised, the bleeding was very difficult to stop. Ryan took injections of the clotting substance to help him live a normal life. Unfortunately, Ryan contracted the AIDS virus from the injections. The virus caused serious problems, beyond the obvious, for Ryan and his family.

"I can't tell you how much being friends with Leslie has enriched our daughter's life. She truly is an exceptional child." **Leslie** has a visual impairment, a hearing impairment, and physical impairments that make moving around school more of a challenge than a freedom. Leslie's friend Karin lives in her neighborhood and has known Leslie all her life. Sometimes Karin wonders about Leslie's disabilities, but most of the time she is too busy playing with Leslie to worry about it.

Students with specific learning disabilities, speech or language impairments, mental retardation, emotional disturbance, deafness and hearing impairments, and visual impairments as well as those who are deaf and blind account for about 95 percent of all students with disabilities in the United States (U.S. Department of Education, 2002). Five additional categories represent the remaining students who receive special education under federally supported programs: multiple disabilities, orthopedic impairments, other health impairments, autism, and traumatic brain injury. In this book, these categories are organized into three groups:

Figure I.1   Relationship of Medical, Physical, and Multiple
Disabilities to Federal Disability Categories

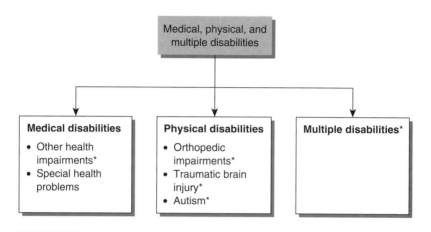

*Categories recognized by federal government

Medical disabilities

Physical disabilities

Multiple disabilities

In the medical disabilities section, we discuss the federal category of "other health impairments" as well as special health problems for which no current special education category exists.

In the physical disabilities section, we discuss orthopedic impairments, autism and other neurological disorders that have physical effects, and traumatic brain injury. Because multiple disabilities is a federal category, we discuss it separately. The way in which we have grouped multiple disabilities is based on what we believe are the central causes and/or primary characteristics of the disabilities. The organization of these topics is presented in *Figure I.1.*

Almost 582,000 students (ages 6–21) with medical, physical, or multiple disabilities received special education services (see *Table I.1*). These students represent about 10 percent of all students with disabilities and about 1 percent of the school-aged population. Their special education needs vary from supportive

Table I.1   Distribution of Students with Medical, Physical, or Multiple Disabilities in the United States

Category	Number	Percentage of All Students With Disabilities
Multiple disabilities	122,559	2.1
Other health impairments	291,850	5.0
Orthopedic impairments	73,057	1.3
Autism	78,749	1.4
Traumatic brain injury	14,844	0.3
Combined	**581,059**	**10.1**
Disabilities in other categories	5,194,663	89.9
All disabilities	5,775,722	100.0

Source: U.S. Department of Education (2002), Table AA2.

consultation provided by related services personnel to very specific assistance related to medical conditions.

Despite low prevalence, there has been heightened interest in medical, physical, and multiple disabilities over the past few years, and heightened activity in the fields of medicine and education to prevent and treat them. Improved medical care has increased the longevity of those with serious illness, adding to the visibility of their conditions. Also, the work of parents and advocacy groups has been especially intense on behalf of those with these low-prevalence conditions.

The same legal and legislative initiatives that have had an impact on the delivery of services to those with higher-prevalence conditions have affected the education and treatment of those with medical, physical, and multiple disabilities. And those initiatives have brought these students into general education settings, increasing their visibility and public interest in their conditions. Finally, the high cost of educating and treating these students has policymakers and educators examining programs and services.

1

What Are Medical Disabilities?

A ll medical disabilities are similar in that they are caused by disease or health problems prior to, during, or after birth. Federal guidelines place students with medical disabilities under the category of "other health impairments." Students in this category have limited strength, vitality, or alertness that adversely affects their educational performance. These limitations are caused by chronic or acute health problems such as heart conditions, tuberculosis, rheumatic fever, nephritis, asthma, sickle-cell anemia, hemophilia, epilepsy, lead poisoning, leukemia, and diabetes. For the most part, the "other health impairments" category includes chronic diseases that affect the whole body. For example, students with attention deficit hyperactivity disorder (ADHD) are eligible for special education services under the "other health impairment" category if problems of limited alertness negatively affect academic performances.

IDENTIFICATION BY MEDICAL SYMPTOMS

The term "other health impairments" tells us little about the educational needs of students. The specific conditions included within the category usually can be identified objectively because of their medical symptoms. Asthma, tuberculosis, and sickle-cell anemia are medical problems that are identified by specific tests. Although the causes of asthma are unknown, the symptoms of labored breathing, shortness of breath, coughing, and wheezing have medical origins: tightening of the muscles around the bronchial tubes as well as swelling of the tissues and increased secretions in these tubes. Tuberculosis is caused by a bacterium that can be identified. Sickle-cell anemia is easy to identify by the shape of the individual's red blood cells (sickle shaped), which impair circulation and result in chronic illness, long-term complications, and premature death.

PREVALENCE OF MEDICAL DISABILITIES

About 291,850 students with "other health impairments" receive special education services (U.S. Department of Education, 2002). This number represents a large increase over previous estimates, largely due to the increased identification of students with ADHD. Students with "other health impairments" represent less than 1 percent of school-aged children and adolescents and about 5 percent of students with disabilities. There is little variation in the percentage of these students identified in each of the states.

"OTHER" HEALTH IMPAIRMENTS

Any illness that interferes with learning can make a student eligible for special services under the category of "other health impairments." This category includes not only those impairments specified in the federal definition (see *Table 1.1*), but also heart conditions, cystic fibrosis, AIDS, and other diseases. Students whose problems are primarily due to alcoholism or drug abuse are not classified with "other health impairments" or any other special education condition even though these problems present special areas of concern for students, teachers, parents, and other professionals.

Table 1.1   Description of Selected Other Health Impairments

Condition	Description
Asthma	Chronic respiratory condition characterized by repeated episodes of breathing difficulties, especially while exhaling
Diabetes	A developmental or hereditary disorder characterized by inadequate secretion or use of insulin produced by the pancreas to process carbohydrates
Nephrosis and nephritis	Kidney disorders or diseases caused by infections, poisoning, burns, accidents, or other diseases
Sickle-cell anemia	Hereditary and chronic blood disease (occurring primarily in people of African descent) characterized by red blood cells that are distorted and that do not circulate properly
Leukemia	Disease characterized by excessive production of white blood cells
Lead poisoning	Disorder caused by ingesting lead-based paint chips or other substances containing lead
Rheumatic fever	Disease characterized by painful swelling and inflammation of the joints that can spread to the heart and central nervous system
Tuberculosis	Infectious disease that commonly affects the lungs and may affect other tissues of the body
Cancer	Abnormal growth of cells that can affect any organ system

Heart Conditions

Heart conditions are not uncommon among young people. They are characterized by the heart not circulating blood properly. Some **heart conditions** are congenital (present at birth); others are the product of inflammatory heart disease (myocarditis, endocarditis, pericarditis, rheumatic heart disease). Some students have heart valve disorders; others have disorders of the blood vessels. Recently, students have been returning to school following heart transplants. When heart disorders or the medications necessary to treat them interfere with a student's ability to participate in normal activities, special education services may be provided as a short- or long-term support system.

Cystic Fibrosis

Cystic fibrosis is a hereditary disease that affects the lungs and pancreas. Those who have cystic fibrosis have recurrent respiratory problems and digestive problems, including abnormal amounts of thick mucus, sweat, and saliva. Students with cystic fibrosis often spend a significant amount of time out of school. The disease is progressive, and few who have it live beyond age 20.

Acquired Immune Deficiency Syndrome (AIDS)

AIDS (acquired immune deficiency syndrome) is a potentially fatal syndrome caused by the human immunodeficiency virus (HIV). HIV is transmitted through body fluids (e.g., through transfusions, unprotected sex, sharing of hypodermic needles, birth from an infected mother). The term AIDS is often applied incorrectly. People with HIV do not necessarily have AIDS. AIDS is a late stage in a series of stages of HIV infection.

Acquired means AIDS is not genetically inherited (many diseases of immune deficiency are) but acquired from some substance or microorganism outside the body. **Immunodeficiency** means that the immune system has been weakened. A **syndrome**

is not so much a disease as it is a collection of symptoms. The effects of HIV infection include susceptibility to additional infections, developmental delays, central nervous system damage, motor problems, psychological problems, and death.

Many teachers are concerned about the risk of working with students with AIDS and other transmittable diseases. Generally, people with medical disabilities require treatments to protect their health and that of those around them. Extreme concern is usually unwarranted, and a few general, common-sense considerations are all that is required beyond the ongoing medical treatments being administered by physicians and other health personnel. Although medical guidelines for preventing the transmission of HIV may continue to be refined, Crocker and Cohen (1988) offer the following relevant tips for allaying concerns about HIV and AIDS:

1. Transmission of HIV in the course of providing usual developmental services should not be a concern.

2. Activities and handling of people with HIV should involve normal interactions consistent with their developmental status and personal health.

3. Caution is required relative to susceptibility to other diseases by people with HIV infection.

4. Good hygienic practices appropriate in all situations of disease or infection require improved attention relative to HIV.

Hemophilia

Hemophilia is a hereditary disease in which the blood clots very slowly or not at all. The disorder is transmitted by a sex-linked recessive gene and nearly always occurs in males. Those who have hemophilia bleed excessively from minor cuts and scrapes and suffer internal bleeding when they are bruised. In recent years, children with hemophilia and their families have faced increasing problems as a result of the potential contamination of blood and blood products with HIV. Students with hemophilia should be protected from contact sports and school activities in which they might suffer a physical injury, but normal physical exercise should be encouraged.

SPECIAL HEALTH PROBLEMS

Special health problems related to alcoholism and drug abuse are not considered disabilities even though they may adversely affect school performance.

Fetal Alcohol Syndrome

Fetal alcohol syndrome occurs in babies born to mothers who drink alcoholic beverages before and during pregnancy (Conlon, 1992). Children born with **fetal alcohol syndrome** have low birth weight and height, have unusual facial features, and evidence mental retardation. Some also have heart problems and varied learning problems.

Alcohol consumed during pregnancy affects the fetus because it crosses the placental membrane. This means that when the mother drinks, the fetus drinks. Some effects of drinking alcohol are decreased protein synthesis, impaired cellular growth, decreased production of essential metabolic products, and inhibited development of nerves (Conlon, 1992). These effects explain the growth retardation, abnormal physical appearance, and other problems of children with fetal alcohol syndrome.

Maternal Cocaine Use

Although not as common as maternal alcohol use, cocaine use during pregnancy receives a great deal of press because it places pregnant mothers as well as their babies at risk for a variety of serious, sometimes life-threatening health problems. Problems for the mothers include seizures, shortness of breath, lung damage, nasal membrane burns, respiratory paralysis, cardiovascular problems, anorexia, and premature labor (Smith,

1988). Although data are limited, it appears that children born of cocaine-addicted mothers experience a variety of problems with significant ramifications for success in school, including increased irritability, elevated respiratory and heart rates, neurological damage, low birth weight, and disturbed sleep patterns. Current information on the long-term effects of maternal cocaine use on children is equivocal: Some argue the effects are permanent and irreversible, and others believe the initial problems can be successfully treated without lasting damage. One thing is sure—babies are being born to mothers who use cocaine, and concern for them and others with health impairments touches every school district in the U.S.

MEDICALLY FRAGILE AND TECHNOLOGY DEPENDENT GROUPS

In recent years, two new groups of students have emerged, each with unique educational needs confounded by serious medical problems. The first group, direct recipients of advances in health care that have improved survival rates, are sometimes referred to as **medically fragile**. The Council for Exceptional Children (1988) defined this group as "those who require specialized technological health care procedures for life support and/or health support during the school day" (p. 12). The second group, sometimes called **technology dependent**, relies on life-sustaining medical equipment and complex nursing care to avoid death or further disabilities (Levy & Pilmer, 1992; Liles, 1993). Four groups of children have been identified as being technology dependent, but the boundaries can be blurred (Liles, 1993):

> Group I Dependent at least part of each day on mechanical ventilators (machines that help them breathe).
>
> Group II Require prolonged intravenous administration of nutritional substances or drugs.
>
> Group III Daily dependence on other device-based respiratory or nutritional support, including tracheotomy tube care, suctioning, oxygen support, or tube feeding.

Group IV Prolonged dependence on other medical devices that compensate for vital body functions, daily or near-daily nursing care. (p. 2)

The diversity of responses to medical problems sometimes makes it difficult to distinguish technology dependent students from the larger group of students with special health problems or other medical disabilities. Generally, as the level of a student's disability improves and the intensity of medical intervention decreases, how the student is classified depends on the response to treatments. For example, should a student whose breathing problems improve over time be called "technology dependent" because he once needed a ventilator to overcome a problem with breathing? Similarly, some students require minimal medical equipment but a great deal of nursing care (e.g., for uncontrolled diabetes), while others may need specialized equipment but limited supervision (e.g., overnight intravenous therapy). Deciding in what group to classify a student also presents problems. Regardless, three key components appear to be prominent in school programs that successfully include students with medical disabilities and special health problems (Liles, 1993):

Clear and open communication to share information about resources and reduce fears.

Collaboration between school personnel and representatives from other agencies dealing with health care issues.

Flexibility to accommodate the often highly individualized needs of these students. (p. 1)

2

What Are Physical Disabilities?

Physical disabilities are problems that result from injuries or conditions affecting the central nervous system or other body systems and their related functions. These conditions affect how children use their bodies. Federal guidelines place students with physical disabilities under the categories of orthopedic impairments, traumatic brain injury, and autism. **Orthopedic impairments** involve the muscular or skeletal system, and sometimes the central nervous system, and affect movement and mobility, which in turn adversely affects a student's educational performance. **Traumatic brain injury** refers to a severe head injury that creates chronic physical problems which affect academic, behavioral, and interpersonal performances. **Autism** is a physical disorder of the brain that causes lifelong problems with communication, thought processes, and attention.

ORTHOPEDIC IMPAIRMENTS

Orthopedic impairments are the most common physical disabilities. They generally involve the muscular, skeletal, or central nervous systems and affect movement and mobility. The term includes impairments caused by congenital anomalies (e.g., clubfoot or absence of some member), impairments caused by disease (e.g., poliomyelitis or bone tuberculosis), and impairments from other causes (e.g., neurological problems, cerebral palsy, amputations, or fractures or burns which cause contractures).

Prevalence

About 73,000 students with orthopedic impairments received special education during the 2000–2001 school year; this number has increased about 40 percent over the previous ten years (U.S. Department of Education, 2002). Students with orthopedic impairments represent less than 1 percent of school-aged children and adolescents and about 1 percent of students with disabilities. There is little variation in the percentage of students identified in each of the states.

SPECIFIC IMPAIRMENTS

Orthopedic impairments limit muscular movement and mobility and vary in their severity. Students with mild impairments can function very well in general education classrooms and require little or no special help. Those with severe disabilities may need special furniture, devices, or the help of trained personnel.

Poliomyelitis

Poliomyelitis is an acute communicable disease caused by the polio virus. The disease can be mild (no apparent symptoms) to severe (paralysis, muscular atrophy, even fatal paralysis). Polio was first recognized in the mid-1800s and became epidemic in Norway and Sweden in 1905. The incidence of polio in North America, Europe, Australia, and New Zealand peaked during the 1940s and early 1950s. A vaccine developed by Dr. Jonas Salk became available in 1955 and virtually eliminated the disease. The Sabin vaccine, which can be taken orally and is more than 90 percent effective, is now the vaccine of choice. Today, it is hard to appreciate how frightening polio once was.

Still, occasional outbreaks of the disease occur, usually among groups who have not been immunized. The most recent outbreak in the United States was in 1979 among Pennsylvania's Amish population.

Muscular Dystrophy

Muscular dystrophy is a group of birth disorders in which the skeletal muscles progressively atrophy; there are no neurological or sensory defects. There are four main forms of muscular dystrophy:

- Pseudohypertrophic (Duchenne's) type accounts for about 50 percent of cases and is found only in boys. It usually is diagnosed when the child begins to walk. The disorder is progressive: By the time they are teenagers, most of those who have the condition use wheelchairs. Few live more than 10–15 years from the onset.
- Facioscapulohumeral (Landouzy-Dejerine) type occurs in both sexes and weakens the shoulders and arms more than the legs. This form usually appears before age 10 but can start during adolescence. Early symptoms include the inability to pucker or whistle and abnormal facial movements when laughing or crying. The disease is slower to progress than Duchenne's type, and many who have the condition live a normal life.
- Limb-girdle dystrophy (juvenile dystrophy or Erb's disease) follows a slow course and often causes only slight disability. Usually the disease begins between ages 6 and 10. Muscle weakness appears first in the upper arms and pelvis. Other symptoms include poor balance, a waddling gait, and an inability to raise the arms.
- Mixed dystrophy generally occurs between ages 30 and 50, affects all voluntary muscles, and causes rapidly progressive deterioration.

Diagnosing any type of muscular dystrophy depends on finding elevated levels of creatine kinase (ck) in the blood. This enzyme is released by dying muscle cells. Currently, there is no treatment to stop the progressive impairment associated with muscular dystrophy. Students who have the condition most often are helped by orthopedic appliances (crutches, walkers, and wheelchairs), exercise, and physical therapy, but it is generally recommended that the use of these aids be avoided as long as possible to encourage maximum use of existing muscle strength.

Juvenile Rheumatoid Arthritis

Juvenile rheumatoid arthritis is a disorder of the tissues that connect bones. The cause is not known. There are three major types of juvenile rheumatoid arthritis: systemic (Still's disease or acute febrile type), polyarticular, and pauciarticular. In the systemic form, the individual develops sudden fevers, rashes, chills, an enlarged spleen and liver, and swollen, tender, and stiff joints. Students with arthritis usually require only mild forms of special education intervention. Students who have severe forms of the disease may be incapacitated for long periods and require in-home instruction.

Osteogenesis Imperfecta

Osteogenesis imperfecta is a hereditary disorder that leaves the child or adolescent with brittle bones. The disease occurs in two forms. In the rarer, fractured bones are present at birth, and the infant usually dies within a few weeks. In the other form (called osteogenesis imperfecta tarda), the child develops fractures after the first year of life. Preventing injury is the most common form of treatment. Depending on the severity of the condition, students either do not participate in contact sports or they wear protective devices (pads, helmets) when they do.

Multiple Sclerosis

Multiple sclerosis is a disease of older adolescence and adulthood. Because students with disabilities are now entitled to a free, appropriate education until age 21, you may come across this condition among your students. Multiple sclerosis is a disease in which the membranes of the brain and spinal cord progressively deteriorate. Those with multiple sclerosis have periods of incapacity and periods of remission, when symptoms are relieved and they can lead more active lives.

Osteomyelitis

Osteomyelitis is an inflammation of the bone marrow. It occurs more often in children than adults, and much more often in boys than girls. Usually, it is the result of an infection coupled with trauma. It begins when a child is bruised in some way and at the same time has an infection. The infection finds a home in the hematoma (swelling) caused by the injury and then spreads through the bone to other parts of the body. In children, the most common infections are in the bones of the arms and legs. Osteomyelitis also can result in underdeveloped bones.

Legg-Calvé-Perthes Disease

Legg-Calvé-Perthes disease is a disorder that affects the head of the femur, the upper bone in the leg. Interrupted blood flow causes the head of the bone to degenerate; a new head forms that is misshapen, usually flattened. The disease occurs most often in boys between the ages of 4 and 10. Those who have the disease show a persistent limp that becomes more severe over time. The disease can interfere with participation in typical class-room activities.

Limb Deficiencies

Limb deficiencies, or loss of one or more limbs, may be present at birth (congenital) or may occur later in life (acquired). A student may be born missing entire limbs or parts of limbs.

Sometimes, because of an accident or illness that requires amputation, a student is missing one or more arms or legs. If the condition interferes significantly with performance in school, the student may receive special education services.

Craniofacial Anomalies

Craniofacial anomalies are defects of the skull and face. Microcephaly (head circumference more than two standard deviations below average), hydrocephaly (accumulation of cerebrospinal fluid in the ventricles of the brain), and cleft palate (gap in the soft palate and roof of the mouth, sometimes extending through the upper lip) are forms of craniofacial anomalies that cause some students to receive special education. For example, one effect of microcephaly and hydrocephaly can be mental retardation. Conditions that involve the mouth or jaw usually result in some form of speech impairment. As a result, craniofacial anomalies can affect the ways people interact with individuals who have them.

NEUROLOGICAL DISORDERS

The neurological (or nervous) system coordinates and directs various body functions (Batshaw & Perret, 1992). Its components are nerves and three subsystems: the central nervous system, including the brain and spinal cord; the peripheral nervous system; and the autonomic nervous system. Each component controls some aspect of behavior and affects how we deal with the world around us. An impairment of any part of this system makes us less able to adapt to the environment and may result in a variety of disorders. Neurological problems can affect the physical structure and functioning of the central nervous system (including the brain or spinal cord) or other components of the nervous system, resulting in neuromuscular problems. Some are genetic; others are due to infection or injury; still others stem from unknown causes.

Epilepsy

Epilepsy affects between 1 and 2 percent of the population. It is characterized by recurring seizures, which are spontaneous abnormal discharges of electrical impulses of the brain. **Petit mal** (or absence) seizures occur most often in children 6–14 years old and usually consist of a brief loss of consciousness (the eyes blink or roll, the child stares blankly, and the mouth moves slightly). Each petit mal seizure lasts from one to ten seconds. Someone experiencing a petit mal seizure simply stares or shows small eye movements like fluttering of the eyelids. **Grand mal** (or tonic-clonic) seizures typically begin with a loud cry, brought on by air rushing through the vocal cords. The person falls to the ground, losing consciousness; the body stiffens, then alternately relaxes and stiffens again. Tongue biting, loss of bowel control, labored breathing, temporary cessation of breathing followed by rapid breathing, and blue to purple coloring of the skin can result. Grand mal seizures generally last for several minutes. Although they can be frightening, they are not dangerous.

Undiagnosed seizures can be mistaken for daydreaming or temper tantrums. Epilepsy can be controlled by medication, which must be monitored to achieve optimal effects. Epilepsy medication has the side effects of drowsiness, lethargy, intellectual dullness, coarsening of facial features, behavioral changes, and sleep disturbances that can also present problems in school. Teachers play an important role in treatment by observing, recording, and reporting behavioral changes that accompany the medical management of epilepsy.

Cerebral Palsy

Cerebral palsy is a group of neuromuscular disorders that result from damage to the central nervous system (the brain and spinal cord) before, during, or after birth. There are three major types of cerebral palsy—spastic, athetoid, and ataxic—although the disorder sometimes occurs in mixed form and other grouping systems are recognized.

Spastic cerebral palsy is the most common, occurring in 70 percent of those who have the disorder. In its mildest form, spastic cerebral palsy can be detected only by a careful neurological examination. Severe spasticity leaves the individual rigid, with muscles tense and contracted. **Athetoid cerebral palsy** occurs in approximately 20 percent of those who have the disorder. The condition results in involuntary movements—grimacing, writhing, sharp jerks—that impair voluntary movements. **Ataxic cerebral palsy** is the rarest form, occurring in about 10 percent of those who have cerebral palsy. Its characteristics include disturbed balance, lack of coordination, underactive reflexes, constant involuntary movement of the eyeballs, muscle weakness, tremor, lack of leg movement during infancy, and a wide gait as the individual begins to walk.

Up to 40 percent of those with cerebral palsy also experience mental retardation, about 25 percent have seizures, and about 80 percent have impaired speech. Cerebral palsy cannot be cured, but proper management or treatment limits further physical damage, improves functional skills, and offers opportunities for increased independence and successful life experiences.

Spina Bifida

Spina bifida is a birth defect that has to do with the development of the embryonic neural tube (the structure from which the brain and spinal cord develop) during the first trimester of pregnancy. One or more vertebrae push the spinal contents out, in an external sac. Usually the defect occurs in the lower back area, but it can occur at any point along the spine. Treatment is a function of the severity of the condition. A student with a minor disorder may require no treatment and may be able to lead essentially a normal life. The most serious form of the condition is **myelomeningocele**. In this form, a saclike structure that contains spinal cord membranes, spinal fluid, and a portion of the spinal cord protrudes over the spinal column. The condition usually is corrected surgically but results in some neurological impairment.

Spinal Cord Injury

Spinal cord injuries occur when the spinal cord is traumatized or partially or totally severed. Spinal cord injuries are

Table 2.1   Types of Paralysis and Their Characteristics

Type	Description
Monoplegia	One limb affected
Paraplegia	Lower body and both legs affected
Hemiplegia	One side of body affected
Triplegia	Three limbs affected, usually legs and one arm
Quadriplegia	All four extremities and trunk affected
Diplegia	Legs more affected than arms
Double hemiplegia	Both halves of the body affected, with one side more than the other

primarily caused by car or motorcycle accidents, gunshot wounds, or falls, although some may be caused by infections. Students with spinal cord injuries will experience partial or total paralysis; the effects depend on the amount of damage and its location. If the spinal cord is completely severed, complete paralysis occurs to a portion of the body. If the spinal cord is partially severed or damaged due to swelling or bleeding following a traumatic injury, partial paralysis will occur. Generally, parts of the body below the spinal cord injury are affected. Each type of paralysis is referred to by a specific term (see *Table 2.1*).

TRAUMATIC BRAIN INJURY

Traumatic brain injury (TBI) is a severe injury to the head that results in a change in the level of consciousness or in an anatomical abnormality of the brain causing physical and cognitive impairments that necessitate special education services (Michaud & Duhaime, 1992). Common causes of head injury include falls, sports- and recreation-related accidents, motor vehicle accidents, and personal assaults, including child abuse. Since the brain is part of the central nervous system, severe injuries to it may have neurological effects. TBI includes scalp and skull injuries, cerebral contusions (bruising of brain tissue), hematomas (blood clots), and concussions (loss of consciousness).

Although scalp injuries sometimes result in considerable loss of blood, they generally have no neurological effects. Of more concern is an injury to the skull referred to as a **skull fracture**. Skull fractures are cracks or broken bones in the skull. They are classified according to both severity and location, and their effects can range from minor to severe. A linear fracture is a crack in the skull bones that is visible on an X-ray; these injuries are usually not associated with neurological problems and are considered less severe than depressed fractures in which the skull bone is broken and presses against the underlying brain tissue. For example, a depressed fracture directly over the part of the brain that controls movement will result in weakness of the opposite side of the body.

Contusions are bruises of the brain tissue that most often result from direct impact to the head. Their effects depend on the extent of the bruise and its location. **Hematomas** are blood clots that form in the brain area. The effects of hematomas depend on their location and type. **Epidural hematomas** form between the skull and the brain covering (i.e., the dura) and may be in arteries or veins. They are sometimes associated with skull fractures that result from falls or from some other impact to the head. The classic sign of an epidural hematoma is a delay in the onset of any symptoms. When the child sustains the injury, the immediate neurological effects appear benign and harmless. As the hematoma enlarges and creates increasing pressure on greater areas of the brain, headaches, confusion, vomiting, and neurological deficits in strength and movement occur. Left untreated, this type of brain injury can be fatal; however, if surgery is performed before the effects are irreversible, the outcomes are very favorable (Michaud & Duhaime, 1992).

Subdural hematomas form beneath the brain covering (i.e., the dura), over the surface of the brain. The symptoms are more severe (e.g., loss of functioning), and the prognosis for recovery is much worse than for epidural hematomas. Subdural hematomas are usually the result of a major generalized injury to the brain.

A brain injury sufficient to cause a brief loss of consciousness or amnesia is called a **concussion**. Usually, concussions are followed in minutes by a complete return to normal mental functioning, although some children experience periods of headaches, drowsiness, and confusion for a couple of hours or even a few days. Most people recover from concussions in 24 to 48 hours.

What should teachers do about traumatic brain injury? Although traumatic brain injury is the number one killer and disabler of American youth, the type of TBI that results in the need for special education is relatively uncommon. About 15,000 students with TBI received special education services during the 2000–2001 school year (U.S. Department of Education, 2002). The primary physical problems associated with head injuries are treated by physicians, emergency room doctors, and other medical personnel. Teachers enter the treatment cycle during rehabilitation phases and aftercare. Consequently, teachers usually provide assistance in overcoming cognitive problems, academic problems, physical problems, behavioral problems, communication problems, and other problems that result from the injury.

Teachers can also play key roles in preventing some of the more serious consequences of head traumas that occur at school (Michaud & Duhaime, 1992). Most head trauma is minor and does not require treatment or result in serious consequences. If a child hits her or his head and does not become unconscious, no treatment is necessary unless symptoms of an epidural hematoma develop. Usually a little "tender loving care" cures minor "bumps on the head." If a child has a severe headache, loses consciousness, shows significant changes in speech or other bodily functions (e.g., vomiting, continuous bleeding), or becomes lethargic, confused, or irritable after a head injury, then medical personnel should be contacted. If a child is momentarily unconscious and then resumes activities, he or she may have a mild concussion. Usually, a neurological exam is recommended after such an incident, and parents are instructed to keep a close watch on the child's behavior, looking for delayed signs of problems (e.g., confusion, cannot be awoken from sleep). Finally, if a child remains unconscious after a fall or head impact, medical personnel should be called immediately.

The National Head Injury Foundation (NHIF) supports the position that most traumatic brain injuries are preventable: The key to prevention is effective education, and the key to effective education is the organization's HeadSmart Schools program. HeadSmart Schools teach safe behaviors and effective coping strategies before unsafe behaviors and poor strategies become bad habits. The HeadSmart Schools program addresses the following areas:

- Pedestrian safety, such as how to walk safely in a crowded neighborhood or across a busy street
- Occupant safety, such as the proper use of safety belts and safety seats
- Tricycle, bicycle, and skateboard safety, such as responsible bike riding in traffic and use of safety helmets
- Playground safety, such as proper surfaces and safe sports equipment
- Alternatives to violence, including child abuse prevention and not shaking a baby. For more information, contact NHIF (see Resources).

AUTISM

According to the National Autistic Society (2002), **autism** is a lifelong developmental disability that affects the way a person communicates and relates to people. Children and adults with autism are unable to relate to others in a meaningful way. Their ability to develop friendships is impaired as is their capacity to understand other people's feelings. People with autism can often have accompanying learning disabilities, but everyone with the condition has difficulty making sense of the world.

Students with autism have impairments in social interaction, social communication, and imagination. This "triad of impairments" is defined as

- Social interaction (difficulty with social relationships, e.g., appearing aloof and indifferent to other people)
- Social communication (difficulty with verbal and nonverbal communication, e.g., not understanding the meaning of gestures, facial expressions, or tone of voice)
- Imagination (difficulty in the development of play and imagination, e.g., having a limited range of imaginative activities, possibly copied and pursued rigidly and repetitively)

In addition to the triad of impairments, repetitive behavior patterns and a resistance to change in routine are common. Autism is a **spectrum disorder**. That is, the symptoms and characteristics of autism can present themselves in a wide variety of combinations, from mild to severe. Although autism is defined by a certain set of behaviors, students can exhibit *any combination* of the behaviors in *any degree of severity.* Two students with the same diagnosis can act differently from each other and have very different skills. Asperger syndrome is a form of autism at the higher functioning end of the autistic spectrum.

Until 1981, autism was included in the definition of severe emotional disturbance, but in that year, the secretary of education moved autism from the federal definition of "severe emotional disturbance" to the category of "other health impairments." The decision to change categories was made in consultation with the National Society for Autistic Children and the National Institute for Neurological and Communicative Disorders and Stroke and was based on evidence that autism was biologically rather than psychologically caused.

Today, autism is a separate category in the federal classification system, and the 1991–92 school year was the first year in which data were collected on the number of children and youth identified with autism. At that time, about 5,200 students with autism were identified (U.S. Department of Education, 1993). Recent figures include more than 75,000 students (ages 6–21) with autism and reflect considerable growth in the identification of these children (U.S. Department of Education, 2001, 2002).

This shift in categories reflects the recurrent debate among professionals about autism. Since Leo Kanner, a psychiatrist at Johns Hopkins University, first brought the disorder to public attention in 1943, professionals have debated the extent to which autism is a biological condition or the result of family, environmental, or psychosocial factors. There is agreement that autism is a complex, brain-based developmental disorder in which multiple areas of functioning are affected. Key symptoms of autism include failing to develop normal socialization patterns; disturbances in speech, language, and communication; unusual relationships to objects and events; unusual responses to sensory stimulation; developmental delays; and onset during the early years of life (Powers, 1989).

Students with autism have difficulties relating to others. They exhibit impaired or delayed speech and language and often repeat words and phrases over and over again (Did you see the movie *Rain Man?*). Sometimes people with autism are over- or under-responsive to sensory stimulation (e.g., light, noise, touch). Sometimes they exhibit inappropriate social and emotional behaviors, and some students with autism engage in repetitive, stereotypic behaviors (e.g., hand-flapping, rocking) that interfere with productive academic and social activities. Many students with autism fail to develop appropriate behaviors related to play, recreation, and leisure. These severe and multiple problems make autism resistant to intervention and treatment.

The primary goals of treatment for children with autism include fostering normal development; promoting learning; reducing rigid, stereotypic behavior patterns; eliminating problem behaviors; and reducing family stress (Hart, 1993; Powers, 1989; Reber, 1992). Programs to address autism that begin early in life (i.e., early intervention programs) are generally the most effective. Essential components of effective programs emphasize functional activities and the skills needed to be successful in the real world, as well as age-appropriate activities, data-based instructional decisions, instruction in school and nonschool environments, and social integration to the maximum extent possible (Egel, 1989). Sue Pratt, president of the Autism Society of America (ASA), believes that people with autism are entitled to the "highest quality of life possible and [should] be treated at all times with the same dignity and respect accorded to everyone else" (Pratt, 1988, p. 2). If you teach students with autism, you may meet professionals who believe that punishment is a necessary component of treatment programs for these students. You may also meet professionals who believe that punishment should not be a part of any treatment program. A resolution, offered by ASA to foster dignity and respect, suggests that strategies based on rewards for engaging in appropriate behavior or refraining from inappropriate behavior rather than punishment should be used as the first line of intervention with students with autism (Egel, 1989). We support practices based on this resolution for all students.

Not too long ago, the prognosis for students with autism was not favorable. Today, opportunities like those available for students with other disabilities (e.g., group living homes) and increasing transition services (e.g., supported employment opportunities) are more common. The keys to successful independent living for students with autism are the same as they are for others with disabilities: fostering independence; providing supportive learning environments; and increasing communication, socialization, and employment skills—in short, treatment as much like neighbors and peers as possible. Holmes (1989) put it this way:

> The concept of "as if" is crucial to ensuring that students are challenged to their full potential. The concept of "as if" is simple: if you treat an adult with autism *as if* he were capable of leading a productive adult life, the chances of him achieving that expectation are greatly improved. On the other hand, if you treat him *as if* he needs constant care, his skills and independence will decline. (p. 257)

This advice can easily be generalized to all students with disabilities (and, probably to most without).

3

What Are Multiple Disabilities?

L eslie Parsons was born with a visual impairment (she is legally blind), moderate hearing loss, cleft palate, muscular imperfection in her extremities, and ptosis (drooping) of the eyelids. She has some difficulty with tasks requiring muscle coordination, fine motor skills, or visual acuity. She wears a hearing aid, which is refitted periodically to accommodate her growth. Every few years, she has an operation to reduce the fluid in her ears. She has had two operations to tighten the muscles in her eyelids. Twice a week, Leslie works with a special education teacher. With the assistance of a device that enlarges and projects print onto a screen, Leslie can read and write independently; she is an outstanding reader.

Students with multiple disabilities, like Leslie, are included in current federal regulations governing special education. The multiple disabilities category is used to identify two types of students:

Those with more than one disability, and

Those with a primary disability and other secondary conditions.

Before the 1978–79 academic year, students with multiple disabilities were not classified. Although they received special education services, they typically were classified as having one or the other of their disabilities. In 1977, the multiple disabilities category was added to federal legislation and formally defined. Today, students with **multiple disabilities** have

> concomitant impairments (such as mentally retarded-blind, mentally retarded-orthopedically impaired, etc.), the combination of which causes such severe educational problems that they cannot be accommodated in special education programs solely for one of the impairments. The term does not include deaf-blindness. (Individuals With Disabilities Education Act, 1990)

Some students with multiple disabilities exhibit such a complex array of symptoms and conditions that it is impossible to identify a primary condition. Others demonstrate a primary disability and a set of other conditions that are severe enough to interfere with placement in classes with students who have a singular disability. Still others, like Leslie, receive special education support primarily in general education classrooms.

Almost 123,000 students with multiple disabilities received special education during the 2000–2001 school year (U.S. Department of Education, 2002). This represents about 2 percent of all students with disabilities. Multiple disabilities was one of the fastest growing categories between 1979–80 and 1991–92, but the growth rate has remained unchanged since that time (U.S. Department of Education, 2000, 2001, 2002).

Why did the numbers in this category change so much? One explanation is that states did not consistently use the same procedures in reporting the number of students with multiple disabilities. Another explanation attributes the fluctuation to decreases in the number of students identified with mental retardation and other health impairments. Students initially identified with mental retardation or other health impairments may have been reclassified as having multiple disabilities when it was recognized that they had related disabilities (e.g., sensory impairments) that required special education. Similarly, increased identification of students with ADHD created dramatic changes in the numbers of students identified as having "other health impairments." It is also possible that some students with mild sensory disabilities are profiting from technological advances that preclude the need for identification with multiple disabilities.

The number of individuals with multiple disabilities has also increased due to advances in medicine and medical technology. Improved prenatal care, lower infant mortality rates, and early diagnosis and treatment all have contributed to the growing number of students with multiple disabilities. Medical advances save lives, in the process prolonging the lives of those whose functioning is significantly limited by multiple disabilities.

Students with multiple disabilities may be more severely impaired than their peers with a single disability. For example, a student with blindness and mental retardation would likely demonstrate severe or profound retardation as opposed to mild retardation. And a student with emotional disturbance and physical disabilities would tend to show more severe problems. Of course, each student is unique. High expectations and special education help students with multiple disabilities live productive, successful lives.

4

What Characteristics Are Associated With Medical, Physical, and Multiple Disabilities?

Students with medical, physical, and multiple disabilities do not demonstrate a set of common characteristics. Their behaviors and characteristics are usually specific to their particular impairments; however some general cognitive, academic, physical, behavioral, and communication characteristics are relevant. Some of the more frequent characteristics that teachers encounter are summarized in the following sections.

COGNITIVE

The cognitive characteristics of students with medical and physical disabilities are specific to particular diseases or injuries. For example, some physical disabilities are accompanied by mental retardation. Students who have a disorder or injury and mental retardation receive the special education services typically received by students with mental retardation. In the same way, students who have an illness or injury as well as learning disabilities usually receive learning disabilities services. One exception is made when a physical disability is so debilitating that school personnel choose to categorize the disability as an orthopedic impairment, placing the student with others who have similar impairments. School personnel usually make these decisions on the basis of available services and programs.

When a condition does not result in mild, moderate, or severe retardation, it is usually classified as an orthopedic impairment or "other health impairment," depending on the classification process used in the school district. These categories do not identify specific cognitive characteristics. In fact, students with motor or speaking difficulties often have no cognitive impairments. This is true, for example, in the case of cerebral palsy.

ACADEMIC

Students with medical or physical disabilities are more likely than their peers without disabilities to experience academic difficulties. The problems are not always a function of academic skills but of limited opportunities to learn, which translate into limited academic achievement. School attendance is a major consideration for some of these students. For example, students with orthopedic impairments may have their school day interrupted by physical and occupational therapy services. Students with other health impairments may not be able to last a full day at school, or may miss school for long periods of time. When students' opportunities to participate in class are limited, they miss academic content. As a result, their grades may suffer.

Increasingly, medical and educational personnel are becoming concerned about the ways in which allergies and medications affect academic performance. For example, the most commonly prescribed asthma medication is correlated with inattentiveness, hyperactivity, drowsiness, and withdrawn behavior. Considerable research is under way on this topic, but the findings to date do not show a clear relationship between allergies and academic performance or between various medications and academic performance.

PHYSICAL

The physical symptoms of students with medical or physical disabilities are specific to their conditions. As with "specific impairments," this category is heterogeneous. Physical problems are the primary difficulties faced by students with orthopedic or other health impairments. For some, disorders mean chronic illness, weakness, and pain; for others, symptoms are present only during acute phases. Some students with medical and physical disabilities develop extraordinary physical strength. Witness the outstanding athletic achievements and upper-body strength of many students who use wheelchairs.

BEHAVIORAL

There are no specific social or emotional behaviors associated with medical or physical disabilities. The social and emotional behaviors that are exhibited are a function of two factors: the specific nature of the condition and its severity. Reactions of parents and other caregivers, as well as of teachers and students, influence the social and emotional behaviors these students exhibit in school, at home, and in the community.

Any physical disability affects the expectations that parents and others hold for the development of a child. Most psychologists agree that the development of healthy social and emotional behaviors depends to a large extent on children's participation in positive interactions with and positive feedback from caregivers. What happens, then, to children with medical or physical problems who are hyperirritable or nonresponsive? How do they interact positively with caregivers?

Clearly, orthopedic impairments create special challenges. Most psychologists recognize the importance of movement in the development of social and emotional behaviors. Young children must move about to learn to be independent and to interact with other young children. Limited motor skills and self-help and self-care skills can restrict students' social interactions. Being restricted from social and school activities also can impede the social and emotional development of students with other health impairments.

Disrupted social development is one of the distinctive features of autism. Individuals with autism often repeat verbatim what others say to them or carry on elaborate conversations that have little or nothing to do with the social context they are in; and they may exhibit aggressive behaviors, self-injurious behaviors, temper tantrums, and repetitive stereotyped behaviors (head rocking, ritualized routines). These behaviors tend to isolate students with autism from their peers, further limiting their social interaction and development.

Many students with medical or physical disabilities also have limited language and communication skills, which can restrict their social and emotional interactions with others. And, these students, like other students with disabilities, have to deal with the attitudes and expectations of others. When expectations are low, they may inhibit social and emotional development. For example, many students with orthopedic or other health impairments demonstrate atypical behavior in response to the expectations of those around them. Those who experience chronic pain can develop emotional reactions to the pain. Those who are terminally ill must deal with the anxiety of death.

COMMUNICATION

The language and communication behaviors associated with medical or physical disabilities are open to few generalizations. Think for a moment about the different forms of cerebral palsy and the degrees of severity within them. Many individuals with cerebral palsy have little language involvement; their speech and language skills are normal. Others are unable to communicate through normal channels. They must use special assistive, augmentative, or alternative systems to communicate. For example, some students with cerebral palsy use **communication boards** (lap-held or wheelchair-held boards that display letters, words, and symbols) to communicate with others.

Individuals with autism usually develop language very slowly. Many never develop functional speech, and those who do show various disturbances—echolalia (repetition of what has been said), saying words or phrases out of context, and voice disorders. They also have poor language comprehension and difficulty following instructions and answering questions.

The cognitive, academic, physical, behavioral, and communication characteristics of these students are those associated with the specific conditions that make up the multiple disabilities. For example, students who have both hearing impairments and learning disabilities are expected to demonstrate the characteristics associated with hearing impairment and learning disabilities, but they might demonstrate at least some of those characteristics at a greater level of severity than those with only one disability.

5

What Should Every Teacher Know About Teaching Students With Medical, Physical, and Multiple Disabilities?

B ased on guidelines established under Part B of the Individuals With Disabilities Education Act (1990) and Section 504 of the Rehabilitation Act (1973) students with disabilities are entitled to a free, appropriate public education that includes specially designed instruction and related services. For students with medical, physical, and multiple disabilities, these related services are often the supports they need to get to and from school and to help them stay in school during the day (Liles, 1993). If the service must be provided by a physician, it is not the school's responsibility. If the service could be provided by a teacher or assistant with minimal training, the school is almost always responsible for providing it. Who shall provide services between these extremes is generally determined during individualized education program (IEP) planning meetings.

IDENTIFYING DISABILITIES

Most students with medical, physical, or multiple disabilities are identified prior to school entry. Sometimes, however, their disabilities commence during the school years. For these students and their families, teachers become valuable resources in helping to identify other health impairments, orthopedic impairments, or other disabilities. Signs they often recognize include limited energy, frequent absences, poor coordination, frequent accidents, speech or language difficulties, mental lapses, and complaints of acute or chronic pain.

Although some of the problems presented by students with medical and physical disabilities can be serious, as a group, people with these disabilities represent a relatively small number of the students receiving special education. Even so, the chances are good that you will have a student with a medical or physical disability in your classroom sometime in your teaching career. Some general tips for teachers of these students are presented in *Table 5.1*. Additional information about instructional approaches and activities follows.

ASKING QUESTIONS

The first step teachers of students with medical and physical disabilities should take is to ask questions to learn about students' needs (see *Table 5.2*). Information should be used to plan instruction and to inform other teachers and students of any special considerations that must be taken. Medical personnel, including the school nurse or the student's physician, can be helpful resources when gathering information and conveying the essentials of it to others. Often, older students or siblings want to convey the information; this practice should be encouraged, but it is a good idea to go over the presentation with the student or sibling before the class hears it to ensure accuracy and that abilities as well as disabilities are discussed.

Table 5.1   Top Ten Tips for Teachers of Students With Medical, Physical, and Multiple Disabilities

1. Ask questions about medical and physical needs.

2. Ask questions about ongoing medical and physical interventions (e.g., medications, physical therapy).

3. Learn to recognize signs of medical or physical distress.

4. Communicate information about needs and distress to all class members.

5. Keep classroom and school work areas accessible.

6. Keep work materials accessible, and make adaptations when necessary.

7. Modify assignments to accommodate medical and physical needs.

8. Have emergency instructions and telephone numbers readily available.

9. Teach emergency procedures to all class members.

10. Recognize limitations, but don't be ruled by them; hold high expectations for *all* students.

Table 5.2   Top Ten Questions for Teachers of Students With Medical, Physical, and Multiple Disabilities

1. Does the student take medication? How often? How much? At school? Any expected side effects? Any other side effects?

2. When and how does the student arrive at school? Any mobility concerns when at school?

3. Does the student require assistance relative to classroom transitions? Any special concerns relative to wheelchair, crutches, or other prostheses?

4. Are there any verbal communication problems? Special communication needs and aids?

(Continued)

Table 5.2 (Continued)

5. Are there any special considerations relative to written communication?

6. Does student require assistance relative to self-care activities (e.g., feeding, dressing, toileting)?

7. Is any special equipment required for self-care?

8. Does the student require positioning aids (e.g., pillows, braces, wedges)?

9. Are there any positions that are preferred for academic or other activities?

10. Is there any other information teachers or other students should have in order to make educational experiences successful?

Source: Berdine and Blackhurst (1985).

IDENTIFYING KEY AREAS OF ASSISTANCE

Some students with medical or physical disabilities may need assistance with their medication while they are at school. Most schools have policies on the administration of medication. Teachers need to be familiar with these policies if medications are being used to control the medical or physical disabilities of students. Students experiencing physical symptoms (e.g., paralysis) may need to be moved from place to place or positioned to benefit from instruction. Others may have seizures and require assistance and care. Medical personnel, including physicians, nurses, physical therapists, and occupational therapists, are valuable resources for providing information and training in these areas. Key additional areas for teachers of students with medical and physical disabilities involve adapting instruction to accommodate individual needs, facilitating communication, and fostering independence.

Bringing Learning to Life: Information Helped Martin's Teachers Allay Concerns About Seizures

One of the characteristics associated with Martin's cerebral palsy was seizures. Although the seizures were being controlled by medication, Martin's teachers wanted information about what to do if he had a seizure at school. His doctor provided them with information describing the steps that are appropriate to assist a person experiencing a convulsive seizure:

- Prevent Martin from hurting himself. Place something soft under his head, loosen tight clothing, and clear the area around him of any sharp or hard objects.
- Do not force any objects into Martin's mouth.
- Do not restrain Martin's movements.
- Turn Martin on his side to allow saliva to drain from his mouth.
- Stay with Martin until the seizure ends naturally.
- Do not give Martin any food, liquid, or medication until he is fully awake.
- Be prepared to give artificial respiration if Martin does not resume breathing after the seizure.
- Provide an area, with supervision, for Martin to rest until fully awake.
- Be reassuring and supportive when the seizure is over.
- While a seizure is not a medical emergency, occasionally one may last longer than ten minutes, or a second seizure may occur. These seizures require medical assistance in a properly equipped facility.

Source: Epilepsy Foundation of America (1981), pp. 10, 12; Batshaw and Perret (1992), p. 516.

ADAPTING INSTRUCTION

Architectural obstacles that impede instruction for students with medical and physical disabilities should be removed or at least rendered manageable. For example, one teacher ordered a specially designed desk for a student in her room who needed a wheelchair to get around. Until it arrived, she placed the student's desk on concrete blocks to raise it to a comfortable level. She also found it helpful to keep the classroom arrangement of desks, work areas, and materials as consistent as possible. If structural changes need to be made in the classroom, she notifies students of the changes. The teacher also places students with physical disabilities at the end of the tables or rows of desks to make movement easier. When she teaches students with other health impairments, she becomes familiar with any special equipment or medical needs and periodically checks to be sure the students are safe and being successful.

Bringing Learning to Life: Information Helped Martin's Teachers Allay Concerns About Seizures

One of the characteristics associated with Martin's cerebral palsy was seizures. Martin's doctor advised his teachers to treat him just like the others students in his class, expecting full participation in all school activities when his seizures were controlled. Although the seizures were being controlled by medication, Martin's teachers wanted information about what to do if he had a seizure at school. His doctor provided them with information describing the steps that are appropriate to assist a person experiencing a convulsive seizure:

- When Martin is having a seizure, ease him to the floor and place something soft and flat under his head, loosen any tight clothing around his neck, and clear the area around him of any sharp or hard objects to prevent him from hurting himself.
- It may help to turn Martin on his side to reduce the possibility of choking, but do not restrain him or put or force anything into his mouth when he is having a seizure.

- If possible, keep track of how long the seizure lasts and stay with Martin until the seizure ends.
- Speak calmly and reassuringly as Martin regains consciousness.
- Remember that there is no conscious behavior involved when Martin has a seizure so he should not be punished or made to feel guilty over something he did while having one.

COMMON ADAPTATIONS

Instructional adaptations required for students with medical and physical disabilities vary greatly, depending on the type and severity of the student's impairment. Some students require specialized assistance throughout the day. Others need support during specific activities only. Still others require only minimal adjustments, such as more time to finish an assignment or a modified response form, to be successful. Some common modifications teachers make to help students with medical and physical disabilities respond to academic tasks include

- Writing on a loose-leaf or spiral-bound notebook, or pad of paper, rather than on a single, loose sheet,
- Securing papers to work areas with tape, clipboards, or magnets,
- Limiting response options to single words or multiple-choice items that require minimal writing,
- Placing rubber strips or pads on work materials (e.g., rulers, calculators, science equipment) to prevent slipping during use,
- Using writing instruments that require less pressure to produce marks (e.g., felt-tip pens, soft lead pencils),
- Adding adaptive devices (e.g., rubber bands, plastic wedges, plastic tubing) to writing instruments to make them easier to grip,

- Using typewriters, word processors, computers, and calculators as substitutes for handwritten responses or calculations, and
- Using study buddies to compensate for activities that require extensive writing.

Modifications that facilitate reading include book holders; reading stands for use while reclining, sitting, or standing; and automatic page turners that can be operated by students with orthopedic impairments with minimal mobility. Audio books allow students who cannot hold books to enjoy a wide variety of reading material.

FACILITATING COMMUNICATION

Some students with medical and physical disabilities require special devices to help them communicate. The most common alternative methods for expressive language are communication boards and electronic devices with synthesized speech output. At the high end of adaptive technology, students use sophisticated equipment to create synthetic speech that teachers and classmates can readily understand. These electronic speech devices are usually operated by typing on a keyboard, by depressing a switch or key, or by touching a pressure-sensitive area of the device. In other cases, the simplest kind of equipment proves useful: Teachers construct boards with hand-drawn pictures representing specific things that the student needs to communicate. Students use the boards by pointing a finger, fist, or object toward the appropriate symbol. Some students, who have limited use of their hands, use a head-mounted pointer or mouth stick to move around the communication board or electronic keyboard. Others use their eyes to localize letters, words, or symbols when communicating. Sometimes special overlays are used in specific content areas (e.g., mathematics symbols or elements of the periodic chart). Speech and language pathologists, parents, and medical professionals generally provide training in the use of such devices.

Bringing Learning to Life: Martin's Teachers Adapted Instructional Activities to Assist Him

Martin's cerebral palsy caused him to have poor motor coordination and inadequate control of his muscles. He had difficulty writing and completing tasks requiring fine motor coordination. Here are some ways his teachers helped Martin to be successful in their classrooms:

- They taped Martin's writing paper to his desk to keep it from moving if his hand or arm brushed it.
- They attached his pencil to his desk with a string so he could retrieve it more easily if he dropped it or knocked it off his work area.
- They used a buddy system to get handouts and assignments to Martin's desk.
- They allowed Martin to dictate answers rather than write them down.
- They provided modified test questions that required short answers, true-false answers, or yes-no answers rather than elaborate, full-sentence responses.
- They used study buddies to provide Martin with lecture notes.
- They gave Martin a little extra time to get ready for class work, to complete class work, and to get from one task or class to another.

Computers with word processing programs and enhanced keyboards, and adaptive writing aids are used to facilitate written communication. Students with orthopedic impairments that cause muscle weakness, involuntary movements, and poor coordination benefit from hand splints or special pencil holders that help them grasp writing instruments. Sometimes, they use slanted boards to support their arms when writing or heavy-weight paper with wide lines to allow extra space for written responses. Computers with keyboard adaptations or voice-activated input are increasingly popular as writing alternatives for students.

FOSTERING INDEPENDENCE

A **prosthesis** is an artificial replacement for a missing body part (e.g., an artificial leg). An **orthosis** is a device that enhances partial functioning of a body part (e.g., a leg brace). An **adaptive device** for daily living is an ordinary item found in the home, office, or school that has been modified to make it more functional for a person with a disability (e.g., a plate with suction cups to hold it to the table and with a rim around it to keep the food from being pushed off). Prostheses, orthoses, and adaptive devices help people with medical and physical disabilities be independent.

Residual Functioning

Students with medical and physical disabilities have skills and abilities, referred to as **residual functioning**, that can help them be more independent. Prosthetics, orthotics, and adaptive devices for daily living often take advantage of residual functioning. For example, an artificial hand is operated by muscles of the arm, shoulder, or back. A person with lower body paralysis uses his or her arms to get around in a wheelchair. Residual functioning helps people with medical and physical disabilities focus on what they can do rather than on what they can't do.

Striking a Balance

Students with medical and physical disabilities have a wide range of personal and social characteristics that can make them dependent on others. Effective teachers help students see that disabilities are just an aspect of life. They allow students with medical and physical disabilities to talk about their limitations, but they encourage them to showcase their abilities as well. Teachers use group activities to encourage socialization among students with disabilities and their peers. Like teachers working with students with sensory disabilities, these teachers are aware of the delicate balance that exists between needing special assistance and wanting to be normal. They are concerned with the impressions a student's special learning needs create, and they try to maximize the extent to which a student is treated positively because of them.

6

Medical, Physical, and Multiple Disabilities in Perspective

The first day of school is tough for many students, while graduation is a time for all to celebrate their accomplishments. Having medical, physical, or multiple disabilities doesn't make these transitions more difficult or more enjoyable. Like their peers, students with disabilities are capable of achievement and deserving of respect. Deciding where students should be cared for continues to trouble teachers, parents, and students. Of concern to many is the question of home versus hospital care.

HOME VS. INSTITUTIONAL CARE

Most professionals agree that home care is more effective in promoting psychological and emotional health. With the rapid introduction of sophisticated home-care technologies, there is no reason to believe that natural settings cannot be equally as effective in promoting physical health. According to Liles (1993), the effectiveness of home care is influenced by factors within the family (e.g., abilities and attitudes) and factors outside the family (e.g., availability of trained personnel and special equipment): "A crucial condition for effective home care is that the family wants the child at home and that it is willing and able to help care for the child or to accept and support a professional, full-time caregiver into the household" (p. 4).

INCLUSION

A crucial condition for effective schooling is that teachers want children with disabilities at school and that they are willing and able to teach and care for the children and to accept support from professionals with expertise related to their disabilities.

Children with medical, physical, or multiple disabilities are entitled to free, appropriate public education, just like their neighbors and peers. Barriers to providing these services include a lack of adequate funding, a lack of public and staff awareness, inadequate services, an inadequate supply of personnel, teachers who don't understand the students' needs, and misinformation about the problems facing these students (Lynch, Lewis, & Murphy, 1993). Strategies for overcoming these barriers are presented in *Table 6.1.* These strategies can help you overcome barriers to providing services to students with disabilities, not just to those with chronic health problems.

Some believe that having students with medical and physical disabilities in general education classrooms creates problems because teachers are uncomfortable teaching these students. They argue that specialized skills are required to meet medical and physical needs and that the extra time required by some students jeopardizes the instruction being provided to others. They think it is more cost-effective to have special equipment required by some of these students centralized and that the expense of making all schools accessible for a few students with medical and physical disabilities is difficult to justify. And, it was not so long ago that arguments such as these were used to segregate most students with disabilities in separate facilities rather than integrate them into classes with their neighbors and peers.

There is no magic bullet for meeting the needs of students with medical, physical, or multiple disabilities. But, what parents said when they were asked what advice they would give teachers is revealing: Treat the child normally, be better informed about the illness and its implications, communicate with families,

Table 6.1   Solutions to Barriers Faced by Students With
Chronic Health Problems

District-Identified Solutions

Change funding procedures to provide incentives for serving
students with chronic health problems.

Ensure school sites are accessible.

Designate responsibility for programs for students with
chronic health problems.

Support hiring of school nurses and make other medical
personnel available to provide assistance with medical
management to teachers and school staff.

Develop ways to hire teachers on nontraditional contracts to
provide assistance after school in homes and hospitals.

Use technology (e.g., telephone links, closed-circuit
television) to provide instruction at home or in hospitals.

Increase contact with families and develop resources to
support them.

Family-Identified Solutions

Improve schools in general, so all students will benefit from
higher quality instruction.

Improve home-based communication.

Allocate funds for educating students with chronic health
problems.

Consider modifications in grading policies and procedures
that are tailored to needs of students with chronic health
problems.

Provide the full range of service delivery options, including
home tutoring and after-school services.

Make information on school and community services
available to families and caregivers.

Serve as resources for parents, families, and other caregivers.

Source: Adapted from information in Table 3 of Lynch, Lewis, and
Murphy (1993).

remain hopeful, build the child's confidence and self-esteem, and be sensitive to the needs of the whole family (Lynch, Lewis, & Murphy, 1993). It is good advice for the teachers of any student.

There is no reason to provide separate education for students with medical, physical, or multiple disabilities. With assistance, these students can be successful in the same classrooms as their neighbors and peers. Evidence to support this belief is everywhere:

• Although Martin needs help when moving around school, he requires little other assistance during the school day. He has done very well in the traditional academic classes he has taken, and his grades are high enough that he will likely go to the college of his choice.

• Mavis is quick to point out the ribbons she has won at horse shows and to brag about the friends she has at school. She used to have a problem discussing her disability, but you would never know it now.

• Leslie's class took a field trip to a nature center. At first Leslie was unhappy and wanted to go home because some of the animals were too far back in their cages for her to see. When she sat down on the ground and wouldn't take another step, her friend Karin didn't know what to do. Fortunately, Ms. Klein said it was lunchtime and, as usual, Leslie had to be first in line. Leslie and Karin ate lunch with a couple of other friends under a tall tree. After lunch, Leslie stuck watermelon pits on her cheeks and said she had chicken pox. Karin laughed so much her stomach hurt. On the bus ride home, as she put her head on Karin's shoulder, Leslie yawned, "It was a great trip, wasn't it?" Karin thought Leslie must like having a good friend like her— she knew she was lucky to have a good friend like Leslie.

Point of View:
Ryan White Taught Us Something

Ryan White died from AIDS in April of 1990. His story was widely publicized as an illustration of the good and bad that sometimes happens to children with disabilities.

In 1984, most people didn't know that Ryan was seriously ill. His mother told some school officials that he had

AIDS in order to explain his many absences from school. In March of 1985, the local newspaper in Kokomo, IN ran a story about Ryan, telling how he and other people with hemophilia had contracted AIDS during their treatments. Ryan's life was changed forever. In August of the following year, he was not allowed to reenter school. Although the school system suggested alternatives (e.g., home tutoring), Ryan's mother refused to go along with them. His family filed a lawsuit to force the district to enroll Ryan in his regular school.

Ryan White's story became national news and badly divided the citizens of his hometown. Many supported the Whites, but many who were frightened and angry took it out on Ryan and his family and friends. When a federal court in Indianapolis ordered the school board to readmit Ryan, it was an empty victory. Many parents were still worried and angry; they refused to let their children play with Ryan or let him have a normal life. A year later, his family moved to Cicero, IN to escape the hostility and loneliness they experienced because of Ryan's illness. The citizens of their new hometown treated Ryan like just another kid, and his trials became of a source of inspiration for other people with AIDS and other health impairments. In 1988, Indiana Governor Robert Orr declared a Ryan White Day, honoring Ryan, his family, and his school. Ryan died in April of 1990, but the last years of his life were filled with dignity and respect.

Ryan's story illustrates the difficult and complicated issues that surround all disabilities. Although much is known about these disabilities, sometimes the facts are simply not enough to prevent misunderstandings and mistreatments. Sometimes worry and fear count for more than knowledge, and people with disabilities suffer. We are the future. If things are to be different for people with disabilities, they must be different with each of us. The senseless persecution of people with AIDS, mental retardation, emotional disturbance, learning disabilities, speech and language impairments, autism, or any other perceived or real disability will only stop if we refuse to let senseless persecution happen again.

7

What Have We Learned?

As you complete your study of teaching students with medical, physical, and multiple disabilities, it may be helpful to review what you have learned. To help you check your understanding, we have listed the key points and key vocabulary for you to review. We have included the Self-Assessment again, so you can compare what you know now with what you knew as you began your study. Finally, we provide a few topics for you to think about and some activities for you to do "on your own."

KEY POINTS

▣ Students with medical and physical disabilities represent a relatively small percentage of students receiving special education. Some of these students have other health impairments, some have orthopedic impairments, and some have specific conditions like autism or traumatic brain injury that affect how well their bodies function.

▣ Students with "other health impairments" include those with disabilities related to disease, infections, or other medical problems.

◙ Students with orthopedic impairments include those with disabilities related to mobility and movement.

◙ Students with neurological impairments include those with disabilities related to central nervous system functioning.

◙ Students with traumatic brain injury have experienced a severe injury to the head that results in a change in level of consciousness or an anatomical abnormality of the brain causing physical and cognitive impairments that necessitate special education services.

◙ Students with autism have multiple areas (including thinking, communication, and behavior) that are affected.

◙ People with medical and physical disabilities have specific educational needs. Those related to "other health impairments" focus on medical management. Those related to orthopedic impairments and other physical disabilities focus on communication, movement, and mobility.

◙ The category of "multiple disabilities" includes people with more than one disability and people with a primary disability and other secondary conditions.

◙ With assistance, many students with medical, physical, and multiple disabilities profit from instruction in the same classes as their neighbors and peers.

◙ Adaptations for students with medical, physical, and multiple disabilities range from simple techniques to the use of high-tech devices. Teaching these students means being ready to adapt to their individual needs.

◙ Students with medical and physical disabilities learn much like other students.

KEY VOCABULARY

Adaptive device for daily living is an ordinary item found in the home, office, or school that has been modified to make it more functional for a person with a disability (e.g., a plate with suction cups to hold it to the table and with a rim around it to keep the food from being pushed off).

AIDS (acquired immunodeficiency syndrome) is a potentially fatal syndrome caused by the human immunodeficiency virus (HIV).

Asthma is a chronic respiratory condition characterized by repeated episodes of breathing difficulties, especially while exhaling.

Autism is a physical disorder of the brain that causes lifelong problems with communication, thought processes, and attention.

Cancer is an abnormal growth of cells that can affect any organ system.

Cerebral palsy is a group of neuromuscular disorders that result from damage to the central nervous system (the brain and spinal cord) before, during, or after birth.

Communication boards are lap-held or wheelchair-held devices that display letters, words, and symbols.

Concussion is a brain injury sufficient to cause a brief loss of consciousness or amnesia.

Contusions are bruises of the brain tissue that most often result from direct impact to the head.

Craniofacial anomalies are defects of the skull and face.

Cystic fibrosis is a hereditary disease that affects the lungs and pancreas.

Diabetes is a developmental or hereditary disorder character-ized by the inadequate secretion or use of insulin, which is produced by the pancreas to process carbohydrates.

Epidural hematomas form between the skull and the brain covering (i.e., the dura) and may be in arteries or veins.

Epilepsy is characterized by recurring seizures, which are spontaneous abnormal discharges of electrical impulses of the brain.

Fetal alcohol syndrome is a condition characterized by low birth weight and height, unusual facial features, and evidence of mental retardation.

Grand mal (or tonic-clonic) **seizures** typically begin with a loud cry, brought on by air rushing through the vocal cords, and the individual falling to the ground, losing consciousness with the body stiffening, then alternately relaxing and stiffening again.

Heart conditions are characterized by the heart not circulating blood properly.

Hematomas are blood clots that form in the brain area.

Hemophilia is a hereditary disease in which the blood clots very slowly or not at all.

Juvenile rheumatoid arthritis is a disorder of the tissues that connect bones.

Lead poisoning is a disorder caused by ingesting lead-based paint chips or other substances containing lead.

Legg-Calvé-Perthes disease is a disorder that affects the head of the femur, the upper bone in the leg.

Leukemia is a disease characterized by the excessive production of white blood cells.

Limb deficiencies, or loss of one or more limbs, may be present at birth (congenital) or may occur later in life (acquired).

Medically fragile individuals require specialized technological health care procedures for life support or health support during the school day.

Muscular dystrophy is a group of birth disorders in which the skeletal muscles progressively atrophy; there are no neurological or sensory defects.

Nephrosis and nephritis are kidney disorders or diseases caused by infections, poisoning, burns, accidents, or other diseases.

Orthopedic impairments involve the muscular or skeletal system, and sometimes the central nervous system, and affect movement and mobility, which in turn adversely affect a student's educational performance.

Orthosis is a device that enhances partial functioning of a body part (e.g., a leg brace).

Osteogenesis imperfecta is a hereditary disorder that leaves the child or adolescent with brittle bones.

Osteomyelitis is an inflammation of the bone marrow.

Petit mal seizures usually consist of a brief loss of consciousness (the eyes blink or roll, the child stares blankly, and the mouth moves slightly).

Physical disabilities are problems that result from injuries or conditions affecting the central nervous system or other body systems and their related functions.

Poliomyelitis is an acute communicable disease caused by the polio virus.

Prosthesis is an artificial replacement for a missing body part (e.g., an artificial leg).

Residual functioning refers to the skills and abilities that students with medical and physical disabilities have that can help them be more independent.

Rheumatic fever is a disease characterized by the painful swelling and inflammation of the joints; it can spread to the heart and central nervous system.

Sickle-cell anemia is a hereditary and chronic blood disease (occurring primarily in people of African descent) characterized by red blood cells that are distorted and that do not circulate properly.

Skull fractures are cracks or broken bones in the skull.

Spina bifida is a birth defect that has to do with the development of the embryonic neural tube (the structure from which the brain and spinal cord develop) during the first trimester of pregnancy.

Spinal cord injuries occur when the spinal cord is traumatized or partially or totally severed.

Subdural hematomas form beneath the brain covering (i.e., the dura), over the surface of the brain.

Technology dependent individuals rely on life-sustaining medical equipment and complex nursing care to avoid death or further disabilities.

Traumatic brain injury refers to a severe head injury that creates chronic physical problems which affect academic, behavioral, and interpersonal performances.

Tuberculosis is an infectious disease that commonly affects the lungs and may affect other tissues of the body.

Self-Assessment 2

A fter you complete this book, check your knowledge and understanding of the content covered. Choose the best answer for each of the following questions.

1. Students who have limited strength, vitality, or alertness that adversely affects their educational performance are called

   a. medically fragile

   b. other health impaired

   c. medically impaired

   d. physically impaired

2. The number of students with health impairments receiving special education services during the past ten years has

   a. increased

   b. remained constant

   c. decreased

   d. first decreased then gradually increased

3. Any _____ that interferes with learning and achievement at school can make students eligible for special services under the category of other health impairments.

   a. physical disability

   b. emotional disability

   c. cognitive disorder

   d. disease

4. Charles has a hereditary disease that affects the lungs and the pancreas. He has recurring respiratory and digestive problems. This disease is

   a. muscular dystrophy

   b. epilepsy

   c. cystic fibrosis

   d. multiple sclerosis

5. Tyrell has a hereditary disease that results in his bleeding excessively from minor cuts and scrapes. He also suffers from internal bleeding if he gets a bruise. This disease is

   a. hemophilia

   b. epilepsy

   c. poliomyelitis

   d. multiple sclerosis

6. A group of birth disorders in which the skeletal muscles progressively deteriorate is called

   a. epilepsy

   b. muscular dystrophy

   c. cerebral palsy

   d. polio

7. Students who require specialized technological health care procedures for life support or health support during the school day are called

   a. technology dependent

   b. dependent

   c. medically fragile

   d. medically dependent

8. Individuals who depend on life-sustaining medical equipment and complex nursing care to avoid death or further disabilities are called

    a. technology dependent

    b. dependent

    c. medically fragile

    d. medically dependent

9. Impairments that involve the muscular, skeletal, and possibly the central nervous systems are

    a. orthopedic

    b. traumatic

    c. acquired

    d. voluntary

10. William suffered a severe head injury when he was hit by a car while riding his bicycle. He was not wearing the bicycle helmet that his parents had purchased for him. As a result of that injury, William has had chronic problems affecting his achievement at school, his behavior, and his social skills. This injury is referred to as

    a. orthopedic impairment

    b. traumatic brain injury

    c. acquired immune disorder

    d. craniofacial anomalies

REFLECTION

After you answer the multiple-choice questions, think about how you would answer to the following questions:

- What factors might affect the academic success of individuals with medical disabilities?
- What factors might affect the academic success of individuals with orthopedic impairments?
- What do effective teachers do to provide support for students with medical disabilities?

Answer Key for Self-Assessments

1. b

2. c

3. d

4. c

5. a

6. b

7. c

8. a

9. a

10. b

On Your Own

☑ Find a journal that focuses on students with medical or physical disabilities. Browse the most recent issues in your library, or review the table of contents. Note the types of articles that are included (e.g., research, opinion, practical suggestions). Find at least three articles that describe specific teaching activities that you could use to help students with "other health impairments" be successful in your classroom.

☑ Find a textbook that focuses on students with medical or physical disabilities. Check the references provided in the textbook. Find at least three articles that describe specific teaching activities that you could use to help students with orthopedic impairments be successful.

☑ Imagine that you are a teacher with a student with cerebral palsy. What decisions would you have to make to help this student be successful? What instructional approaches would be appropriate for working with this student? What specific activities would you use to modify a lesson you were teaching to your class on grammar and proper punctuation?

☑ Diagram the content of this book and prepare a three-paragraph description of what you know about medical, physical, and multiple disabilities.

☑ To better understand how people with medical, physical, and multiple disabilities experience the world, try these simulations and note your reactions to them:

  – Use a pair of crutches to move between classes; take what you would normally take with you (e.g., books, notebooks).

- Use a wheelchair to go from the center of a college campus to the library. Locate a couple of books about medical and physical disabilities, and check them out while still in the wheelchair. Do this without speaking.

- Strap one arm behind your back, and go through a cafeteria line; or make a retail purchase using only sign language.

- Have a conversation with a friend, avoiding eye contact and repeating every other sentence said to you.

☑ Look through the Yellow Pages of your phone book for the name of a physical therapist or speech language pathologist. Invite this person to demonstrate the adaptive devices and/or prosthetics and orthotics needed by students with medical or physical disabilities.

☑ Contact a local, state, or national organization that focuses on people with medical or physical disabilities. Identify the purpose of the organization, its membership, and its services.

☑ Observe a professional, other than a teacher, who works with children with medical, physical, or multiple disabilities. Describe what you see and how it relates to classroom instruction.

Resources

Books

Adams, B. (1979). *Like it is: Facts and feelings about handicaps from kids who know.* New York: Walker. A group of young people with disabilities share their problems and adjustments. This is an excellent book for upper elementary and middle school students.

Aiello, B., & Shulman, J. (1990). *It's your turn at bat.* Breckenridge, CO: Twenty-First Century. The "Kids on the Block" puppets tackle cerebral palsy. This is an excellent book for young readers.

Aiello, B., & Shulman, J. (1992). *Friends for life.* Breckenridge, CO: Twenty-First Century. The "Kids on the Block" puppets tackle AIDS, providing another excellent resource for young readers.

Batshaw, M. L. (Ed.). (2001). *When your child has a disability* (2nd ed.). Baltimore, MD: Brookes. This book offers expert advice on a wide range of medical and educational issues as well as detailed coverage of the daily and long-term care requirements of specific medical and physical disabilities, including autism, seizure disorders, spina bifida, and cerebral palsy.

Batshaw, M. L. (Ed.). (2002). *Children with disabilities* (5th ed.). Baltimore, MD: Brookes. This resource provides extensive coverage of the developmental, clinical, educational, family, and intervention issues faced by professionals in their work with children with disabilities.

Batshaw, M. L., & Perret, Y. M. (1992). *Children with disabilities: A medical primer* (3rd ed.). Baltimore, MD: Paul H. Brookes. This excellent sourcebook for parents and professionals includes information about the medical needs of children with disabilities. Causes and effects, diagnostic and intervention strategies, and general information about how organ systems work (and what can go wrong with them) are described.

Bigge, J. L. (1989). *Teaching individuals with physical and multiple disabilities* (3rd ed.). Columbus, OH: Merrill. This is a comprehensive examination of problems faced by people with physical disabilities, and includes chapters on assessment, instructional methods, and curriculum components.

Blume, J. (1974). *Deenie.* Minneapolis, MN: Bradbury. Instead of becoming a model, as her mother wishes, Deenie must cope with physical problems and wearing a spinal brace. This is an excellent read for upper elementary and junior high school students.

Brown, T. (1984). *Someone special, just like you.* New York: Holt, Rinehart, and Winston. This book for preschoolers and young children was written to help them accept and become more comfortable with children with disabilities.

Cassie, D. (1984). *So who's perfect! People with visible differences tell their own stories.* Scottdale, PA: Herald Press. This excellent compilation of the experiences of people with disabilities includes the stories of people with cerebral palsy, muscular dystrophy, spina bifida, and other health and orthopedic impairments.

Fanshawe, E. (1975). *Rachel.* Scarsdale, NY: Bradbury. Rachel enjoys life and participates fully in many activities at home, at school, and on vacation, illustrating similarities between people with disabilities and their peers.

Geralis, E. (Ed.). (1991). *Children with cerebral palsy.* Rockville, MD: Woodbine House, Inc. This resource about cerebral palsy includes chapters on diagnosis, assessment, treatment, early intervention, and family life. It also provides a resource guide with descriptions of national and state organizations.

Greenfield, J. (1972). *A child called Noah.* New York: Harcourt Brace Jovanovich. In 1969, *Life* magazine published Josh Greenfield's account of life with his son Noah. This book, although dated, is an excellent chronicle of five years of life with a child who would grow older but "not grow up" and for whom no cure was available.

Hart, C. A. (1993). *A parent's guide to autism.* New York, NY: Pocket Books. This is a well-written resource describing symptoms and types of autism, possible causes, therapy options, treatment alternatives, and other important information for parents and other professionals.

Hermes, P. (1991). *What if they knew?* New York: Harcourt. Jeremy has epilepsy and must adjust to living with her grandparents. It is an excellent book for upper elementary school students.

Howard, E. (1989). *Edith, herself.* New York: Macmillan. At the turn of the century, Edith is sent to live with her married sister when their mother dies. Her life there is complicated by epileptic seizures. Upper elementary and junior high school students will enjoy this story.

Kline, F. M., Silver, L. B., & Russell, S. C. (Eds.). (2001). *The educator's guide to medical issues in the classroom.* Baltimore, MD: Brookes. This is a very practical book about collaboration between professionals in educational and medical communities.

Knowles, A. (1983). *Under the shadow.* New York: Harper. Cathy becomes friendly with a boy who has muscular dystrophy. It's a great book for upper elementary and junior high school students.

Krementz, J. (1992). *How it feels to live with a physical disability.* New York: Simon & Schuster. The book tells twelve stories of children aged 6–16 with medical and physical disabilities; it provides photographs that illustrate aspects of daily living in positive ways.

Lynch, V. J. (Ed.). (1999). *HIV/AIDS at year 2000: A sourcebook for social workers.* Boston: Allyn & Bacon. This sourcebook for professionals and families explores current medical, psychosocial, and value and ethics issues surrounding HIV through vignettes that illustrate problems and challenges.

Martin, A. M. (1984). *Inside out.* New York: Holiday. Jonno's younger brother, John, has autism. It is an excellent book for upper elementary and middle school students.

Orelove, F. P., & Sobsey, D. (1996). *Educating children with multiple disabilities: A transdisciplinary approach* (3rd ed.). Baltimore, MD: Brookes. This book offers strategies for transdisciplinary teams working with children with mental retardation and motor or sensory impairments. It includes information about developing an inclusive curriculum, integrating health care and education programs, using assistive technology, planning transitions, and addressing families' needs and concerns.

Phelan, T. (1979). *The S. S. Valentine.* New York: Macmillan. Connie, who uses a wheelchair, is a success in the class play. This is an excellent book for upper elementary school students.

Powers, M. D. (Ed.). (1989). *Children with autism: A parent's guide.* Rockville, MD: Woodbine House, Inc. Recommended as a first book on autism for families, *Children with Autism* includes information about diagnosis, treatment, daily living, education, and legal rights.

Reisner, H. (Ed.). (1993). *Children with epilepsy: A parents' guide.* Rockville, MD: Woodbine House, Inc. This is a superior resource for parents of children who have epilepsy. It includes information about assessment, medical treatment, daily living, and education.

Roberts, W. D. (1987). *Sugar isn't everything.* New York: Macmillan. This story presents the facts about diabetes for young readers.

Rosenberg, M. B. (1983). *My friend Leslie.* New York: Lothrop, Lee, & Shepard Books. This is a sensitive portrait of a young girl and her friend with multiple disabilities during their first year at school. It addresses many questions and feelings that are likely to spring up when children and adults meet a person with a disability for the first time.

Rosenberg, M. B. (1988). *Finding a way: Living with exceptional brothers and sisters.* New York: Lothrop, Lee, & Shepard Books. This is a sensitive, warm, and straightforward exploration of the feelings of three children from different families, each the brother or sister of a sibling with a disability (i.e., diabetes, asthma, and spina bifida).

Roy, R. (1982). *Where's Buddy?* Boston, MA: Houghton Mifflin. Mike must take care of his diabetic brother. Elementary school students will enjoy this book.

Roy, R. (1985). *Move over, wheelchairs coming through!* New York: Clarion Books. Seven young people in wheelchairs talk about their lives with disabilities including cerebral palsy, spina bifida, and muscular dystrophy.

Slote, A. (1973). *Hang tough, Paul Mather.* New York: Harper. Candidly and without sentimentality, Paul recalls from his hospital bed the details of his struggle with leukemia.

Sperry, V. W. (2001). *Fragile success: Ten autistic children, childhood to adulthood* (2nd ed.). Baltimore, MD: Brookes. This uncommon book provides a rare view of autism in all its variations. A former teacher traces the lives of her students over 30 years. The true case histories provide insight into the mystery and diversity of autism—how it affects the students' personal lives, social habits, work, and hobbies and how their conditions change over the years.

Umbreit, J. (Ed.). (1983). *Physical disabilities and health impairments: An introduction.* Columbus, OH: Merrill. This overview offers information on the causes, treatments, prognoses, and educational implications of medical and physical disabilities.

Volkmar, F. (Ed.). (1998). *Autism and pervasive developmental disorders.* New York: Cambridge University Press. This extensive summary of current research on the diagnosis and definition of autism and related conditions discusses genetic and neurobiological factors, drug treatments, and the social disturbance associated with autism.

Wetherby, A. M., & Prizant, B. M. (Eds.). (2000). *Autism spectrum disorders: A transactional developmental perspective.* Baltimore, MD: Brookes. This comprehensive reference provides a thorough overview of the communication, language, social, and behavioral characteristics of autism. Readers gain an understanding of the principles and philosophies behind clinical and educational practices.

Ylvisaker, M. (Ed.). (1985). *Head injury rehabilitation: Children and adolescents.* San Diego, CA: College-Hill Press. This overview provides information on the cause, treatment, prognosis, and educational implications of head injuries.

JOURNALS AND ARTICLES

American Journal of Diseases of Children (AJDC) provides information for physicians and other caregivers on current research developments and clinical findings on pediatric problems likely to occur in day-to-day practice. Contact Editor, *AJDC*, American Medical Association, 536 N. Dearborn Street, Chicago, IL 60610.

American Journal of Occupational Therapy (AJOT). Editor, *AJOT*, Department of Public Policy, George Mason University, 3401 N. Fairfax Drive, Arlington, VA 22201–4498. *AJOT* provides articles about research-based program evaluations, program descriptions, and other research-oriented activities of interest to occupational therapists and teachers working with students with physical disabilities.

Archives of Pediatrics & Adolescent Medicine (APAM). Dr. Frederick P. Rivara, University of Washington, Department of Pediatrics,

P.O. Box 358853, Seattle, WA 98195–8853. *AJDC* provides information for physicians and other caregivers on current research developments and clinical findings on pediatric problems likely to occur in day-to-day practice.

Archives of Physical Medicine and Rehabilitation (APMR). APMR Editorial Office, 330 N. Wabash Avenue, Suite 2510, Chicago, IL 60611–3604. *APMR* is the official journal of the American Congress of Rehabilitation Medicine and the American Academy of Physical Medicine and Rehabilitation. Its purpose is to publish reports of original research and clinical experience in physical medicine and rehabilitation, diagnosis, therapy, and the delivery of rehabilitation care. Contact James S. Lieberman, Editor-in-Chief, APMR, Suite 1310, 78 E. Adams Street, Chicago, IL 60603–6103.

Brain Injury (BI). Jeff Kreutzer, Medical College of Virginia Hospitals, Virginia Commonwealth University, Department of Physical Medicine and Rehabilitation, Richmond, VA 23298. *BI* covers all aspects of brain injury, including basic scientific research, causes, medical procedures, assessment methods, and rehabilitation interventions. Contact Henry H. Medical College of Virginia Hospitals, Virginia Commonwealth University, P.O. Box 677, Richmond, VA 23298.

Developmental Medicine and Child Neurology (DMCN). Editor, *DMCN*, MacKeith Press, High Holborn House, 52–54 High Holborn, London WC1V6Rl, UK. *DMCN* contains research articles and opinion papers of broad interest to those working with people with medical, physical, or multiple disabilities. It was formerly known as *Cerebral Palsy Bulletin.* Contact Editor, *DMCN*, Blackwell Scientific Publications, Osney Mead, Oxford, England OX2 0EL.

Journal of Autism and Developmental Disorders (JADD). Gary B. Mesibov, Editor, *JADD*, Division TEACCH, 100 Renee Lynn Drive, Carrboro, NC 27510. *JADD* is devoted to all severe psychopathologies of childhood and is not necessarily limited to autism and childhood schizophrenia. Experimental studies on the biochemical, neurological, and genetic aspects of these disorders; implications of normal development for deviant processes; interactions between disordered behavior and social or group factors; research and case studies on interventions; and studies related to diagnostic concerns fall within the scope of articles. Contact Eric Schopler, Editor, *JADD*, Department of Psychiatry, CB 7180 Medical School Wing E, School of Medicine, University of North Carolina, Chapel Hill, NC 27599.

Journal of Head Trauma Rehabilitation (JHTR). Editor, *JHTR*, Aspen Systems Corporation, 7201 McKinney Circle, P.O. Box 990, Frederick, MD 21701. *JHTR* provides information on the clinical management and rehabilitation of people with head injuries. Contents are prepared for use by practicing professionals. Contact Editor, *JHTR*, Aspen Systems Corporation, 7201 McKinney Circle, P.O. Box 990, Frederick, MD 21701.

Physical and Occupational Therapy in Pediatrics (POTP). Mary Law, Editor, *POTP*, School of Rehabilitation Science, McMaster University, IAHS Building, 1400 Main Street West, Hamilton, Ontario. *POTP* is designed for physical therapy and occupational therapy pediatric professionals working in hospitals, rehabilitation centers, schools, community settings, and health and human service agencies. It provides the latest clinical research and practical applications for professionals concerned with the physical and occupational needs of people with disabilities. Contact Suzanne K. Campbell, Editor, *POTP*, Department of Medical Allied Health Professions, University of North Carolina, Medical Wing C221 H, Chapel Hill, NC 27514.

Rehabilitation Literature (RL) is a review and abstracting journal with articles pertaining to the care, welfare, education, and employment of people with disabilities. Research papers, opinion pieces, and book reviews are among the typical contents. Most of the material has broad applicability for professionals working in medical and allied health professions as well as in schools and other community agencies. Contact Stephen J. Regnier, Editor, *RL*, 70 East Lake Street, Chicago, IL 60601.

ORGANIZATIONS

Autism Society of America (ASA)

ASA is a national organization of parents and professionals established to promote better understanding of autism, to encourage development of services, to support research, and to advocate on behalf of people with autism and their families. ASA provides information and referral services and publishes the *Advocate,* a bimonthly newsletter. ASA, 7910 Woodmont Avenue, Suite 300, Bethesda, MD 20814–3067.

Division for Physical and Health Disabilities (DPHD)

A division of the Council for Exceptional Children (CEC), formally affiliated in 1958, DPHD promotes quality programs for individuals with physical and/or health impairments. With about 1,700 members, DPHD provides outlets for the exchange of ideas through a variety of resources, including the *DPH Newsletter.* CEC, 1100 North Glebe Road, Suite 300, Arlington, VA 22201–5704.

National Head Injury Foundation (NHIF)

NHIF is a membership organization founded in 1980 by the parent of a person with a severe traumatic brain injury (TBI). Its mission is to improve the quality of life for persons with TBI and their families and to promote prevention. Since its inception, NHIF has grown to 44 state associations with many support groups. It is the leading source of informational materials on this subject in the U.S. Members receive the quarterly newsletter as an update on association news, educational seminars, legislative efforts, the latest research, innovative community programs, international news, and events. NHIF, 1776 Massachusetts Avenue N.W., Suite 100, Washington, DC 20036.

Organizations for Specific Impairments

American Cancer Society, 1599 Clifton Road, Atlanta, GA 30329; (404) 320-3333.

American Diabetes Association, P.O. Box 25757, Alexandria, VA 22313; (703) 549-1500.

Arthritis Foundation, 1314 Spring Street N.W., Atlanta, GA 30309; (404) 872-7100.

Association of Birth Defect Children, 3526 Emerywood Lane, Orlando, FL 32812; (407) 859-2821.

Epilepsy Foundation of America, 4351 Garden City Drive, Landover, MD 20785; (301) 459-3700.

Muscular Dystrophy Association, 810 Seventh Avenue, New York, NY 10019; (212) 586-0808.

National Association for Developmental Disabilities Council, Suite 103, 1234 Massachusetts Avenue N.W., Washington, DC 20005; (202) 347-1234.

National Association for People with AIDS, 2025 I Street, Suite 415, Washington, DC 20006; (202) 429-2437.

National Center for Zero to Three, 2000 14th Street North, Suite 380, Arlington, VA; (703) 528-4300.

National Foundation for Asthma, P.O. Box 300069, Tucson, AZ 85751; (602) 323-6046.

National Information Clearinghouse for Infants with Disabilities and Life Threatening Conditions, Center for Developmental Disabilities, University of South Carolina, Bensen Building, First Floor, Columbia, SC 29208; (803) 774-4435.

National Multiple Sclerosis Society, 205 E. 42nd Street, New York, NY 10017; (212) 986-3240.

National Society for Children and Adults with Autism, 621 Central Avenue, Albany, NY 12206; (518) 459-1418.

Office for Developmental Disabilities Services, Health and Human Services, 349F Hubert H. Humphrey Building, 200 Independence Avenue S.W., Washington, DC 20201; (202) 279-6085.

United Cerebral Palsy Association, 66 E. 34th Street, New York, NY 10016; (212) 481-6300.

References

Americans With Disabilities Act, Pub. L. No. 101-336, 104 Stat. 327 (1990).

Batshaw, M. L. (2002). *Children with disabilities* (5th ed.). Baltimore, MD: Paul H. Brookes.

Batshaw, M. L., & Perret, Y. M. (1992). *Children with disabilities: A medical primer* (3rd ed.). Baltimore, MD: Paul H. Brookes.

Berdine, W. H., & Blackhurst, A. E. (Eds.). (1985). *An introduction to special education.* Boston: Little, Brown.

Berdine, W. H., & Blackhurst, A. E. (Eds). (1993). *An Introduction to Special Education.* (3rd ed.). New York: HarperCollins.

Conlon, C. J. (1992). New threats to development: Alcohol, cocaine, and AIDS. In M. L. Batshaw & Y. M. Perret, *Children with disabilities: A medical primer* (pp. 111–136). Baltimore, MD: Paul H. Brookes.

Council for Exceptional Children. (1988). *Report of the Council for Exceptional Children's Ad Hoc Committee on Medically Fragile Students.* Reston, VA: Author, Governmental Relations Committee.

Crocker, A. C., & Cohen, H. J. (1988). *Guidelines on developmental services for children and adults with HIV infection.* Silver Springs, MD: American Association of University Affiliated Programs for Persons With Developmental Disabilities.

Egel, A. L. (1989). Finding the right educational program. In M. D. Powers (Ed.), *Children with autism: A parent's guide* (pp. 169–202). Rockville, MD: Woodbine House, Inc.

Epilepsy Foundation of America. (1981). *Me and my world.* Landover, MD: Author.

Greer, B. B., Allsop, J., & Greer, J. G. (1980). Environmental alternatives for the physically handicapped. In J. W. Schifani, R. M. Anderson, & S. J. Odle (Eds.), *Implementing learning in the least restrictive environment.* Austin, TX: Pro-Ed.

Hart, C. A. (1993). *A parent's guide to autism.* New York: Pocket Books.

Holmes, D. L. (1989). The years ahead: Adults with autism. In M. D. Powers (Ed.), *Children with autism: A parent's guide* (pp. 253–276). Rockville, MD: Woodbine House, Inc.

Individuals With Disabilities Education Act, Pub. L. No. 101-476, 104 Stat. 1141 (1990).

Levy, S. E., & Pilmer, S. L. (1992). The technology-assisted child. In M. L. Batshaw & Y. M. Perret, *Children with disabilities: A medical primer* (pp. 137–157). Baltimore, MD: Paul H. Brookes.

Liles, C. (1993). Serving children with special health care needs in school. *South Atlantic Regional Resource Center Newsletter, 3,* 1–10.

Lynch, E. W., Lewis, R. B., & Murphy, D. S. (1993). Educational services for children with chronic illnesses: Perspectives of educators and families. *Exceptional Children, 59,* 210–220.

Michaud, L. J., & Duhaime, A. (1992). Traumatic brain injury. In M. L. Batshaw & Y. M. Perret, *Children with disabilities: A medical primer* (pp. 525–546). Baltimore, MD: Paul H. Brookes.

National Autistic Society. (2002). *What is autism?* Retrieved December 21, 2005, from http://www.nas.org.uk/nas/jsp/polopoly.jsp?d= 211.

Powers, M. D. (1989). What is autism? In M. D. Powers (Ed.), *Children with autism: A parent's guide* (pp. 1–29). Rockville, MD: Woodbine House, Inc.

Pratt, S. (1988). Resolution discussed and concerns stated [Editorial]. *Advocate, 20*(4), 2.

Reber, M. (1992). Autism. In M. L. Batshaw & Y. M. Perret, *Children with disabilities: A medical primer* (pp. 407–420). Baltimore, MD: Paul H. Brookes.

Rehabilitation Act, Pub. L. N. 93112, 87 Stat. 357 (1973).

Smith, J. (1988). The dangers of prenatal cocaine use. *American Journal of Maternal Child Nursing, 13*(3), 174–179.

U.S. Department of Education. (1993). *Fifteenth annual report to Congress on the implementation of the Individuals With Disabilities Education Act.* Washington, DC: Author.

U.S. Department of Education. (2000). *Twenty-second annual report to Congress on the implementation of the Individuals With Disabilities Education Act.* Washington, DC: Author.

U.S. Department of Education. (2001). *Twenty-third annual report to Congress on the implementation of the Individuals With Disabilities Education Act.* Washington, DC: Author.

U.S. Department of Education. (2002). *Twenty-fourth annual report to Congress on the implementation of the Individuals With Disabilities Education Act.* Washington, DC: Author.

Index

Note: Numbers in **Bold** followed by a colon [:] denote the book number within which the page numbers are found.

**CORWIN
PRESS**

The Corwin Press logo—a raven striding across an open book—represents the union of courage and learning. Corwin Press is committed to improving education for all learners by publishing books and other professional development resources for those serving the field of PreK–12 education. By providing practical, hands-on materials, Corwin Press continues to carry out the promise of its motto: **"Helping Educators Do Their Work Better."**